JUST HARMLESS FLIRTING

Tessa Daly

978-1-915502-28-5

© 2023 Tessa Daly. All rights reserved.

This book is copyright under the Berne Convention. All intellectual property rights including copyright, design right and publishing rights rest with the author. No part of this book may be reproduced or transmitted in any way including any written, electronic, recording, or photocopying without written permission of the author. This is entirely a work of fiction. Names, characters, businesses, places, events, locales, and incidents are either the products of the author's imagination or used in a fictitious manner. Any resemblance to actual persons, living or dead, or actual events is purely coincidental. Published by Orla Kelly Publishing.

Orla Kelly Publishing
27 Kilbrody,
Mount Oval,
Rochestown,
Cork,
Ireland

I would like to dedicate this book to my friend Pierce McCarthy, who sadly passed away in October 2022. I would also like to thank the men in my life, for looking after me while I wrote and of course Orla Kelly Publishing, without whom this book would not be possible.

Chapter 1

Ruth felt the cold wind whip around her as she waited at Thomastown train station in Co Kilkenny. Her husband had dropped her off on his way to work. Now she had to wait for her friend Alice before they got the train to Dublin on the first leg of the trip.

Ruth and Alice lived in the townland of Barrycastle just outside the town Thomastown in Kilkenny, and this was the first time they were going on holiday without their husbands. As they waited on the platform, there was excitement between them. "Imagine the sun", said Alice. Ruth just smiled and nodded in agreement.

"Yes, after the summer we've had, I can't wait to put my sandals on", said Alice, and she giggled like a child.

"We'll miss the two boys, I suppose", said Ruth, laughing.

"Yes", said Alice, "we will miss them all right, and how will we know what to do or where to eat without them to decide for us?" The women felt free and excited at the prospect of going off on their own.

In their fifties, Alice had her family reared, and Ruth did not have children. They had expected some resistance from their respective husbands when they decided to go on holiday alone. Alice has been married to Tom for twenty-five years, and both of their girls were in college. Tom ran the farm and loved the Gaelic Athletic Association, or GAA. There was always a match or a meeting to go to, so his life was just as he wanted it. Alice, however, often wished there was more, something more than her job at the hospital. She had never voiced this feeling to anyone, not even to Ruth, who seemed content with her husband, Dennis Cullen, a factory manager in Carlow. If asked, she couldn't pinpoint what it was that was missing from her life.

The train was packed with people going to work, and the day looked the same as any other day, but, of course, it wasn't, not for these two women. "Have you got your passport?" said Ruth. "And your boarding pass?" Alice checked once more just to make sure, and so did Ruth. They decided to take the easy option and get a taxi to the airport. Hang the expense, they had two large suitcases and hand luggage as well, and everything they would need for two weeks in the sun.

As they waited for the flight, Ruth got a phone call. She looked at Alice with a hint of dread. "What now?" It was Dennis just checking to make sure that they got there safely. "Yes, we are about to board the flight now. All is well. Okay, bye now. See you in two weeks", she told him.

"Yes, thank God for that. Now get on that plane fast as you can before something happens and we have to go back". Alice laughed loudly as they ran to get in the queue for boarding.

The flight was uneventful, and they passed the time reading and chatting, but the mood changed as they neared their destination. The passengers became excited at the prospect of landing and beginning their holiday.

As they left the plane and walked through to security, they could feel the warmth, and they could only imagine what lay before them: two weeks at the beach, browsing the shops and sunning themselves at the pool.

It was the first time in Lanzarote for both women. As they travelled by taxi to their hotel, they were struck by the landscape that was so different from anything they had seen before: the rocky ground and white houses in the distance, palm trees lining the roads and waving in the warm breeze. As the taxi pulled up outside the hotel, it looked lovely, with white marble steps and flags blowing in the bright evening sunshine. As they waited to be checked in, the heat forced them to shed some of the layers they had worn coming from Ireland.

They were told to take the lift down one floor. "Oh my God", said Ruth. They were in the basement, and a feeling of dread set in as they entered the lift. They looked from one to the other until the lift came to a stop. Stepping out and pulling their luggage after them, it didn't take long to find their room. It was quite dark inside the room, and they had to turn the light on, until they realised that the curtains were closed. Not a word was spoken until Alice went and opened the curtains and the light flooded the entire apartment. The place looked very nice as they went from room to room, and then it was time to check out the view and the balcony. They were blown away to find the pool right outside their room, and the beach just a few steps away.

They walked out the terrace door and looked at each other in silence. Alice broke it when she looked at her friend and said, "Imagine, Ruth, this is our home for the next two weeks".

"Come on", said Ruth, "let's have a look around".

As they went around to the other side of the pool, to their delight they found the beach just through the small gate. There was sand and blue sea as far as they could see.

This was the best location they had ever seen, and they couldn't wait to explore the island.

Chapter 2

After unpacking, they decided to get dressed for the evening and go out. They knew from friends that Puerto Del Carmen was in two parts, new town and old town, but they had no idea how far either one was from the hotel. The lady at reception told them to go right for the new town and left for the old town. She also pointed out that there were lots of Irish bars and restaurants in the old part and it was within walking distance.

Decision made, they would go left, plenty of time to see the whole place. As they made their way up the hill, the women agreed that flat-heel shoes were a wise choice. Alice had almost given up wearing heels. She seldom went someplace special, and she had also put on some weight and found it difficult to walk in them, but she packed a pair anyway.

Ruth on the other hand managed very well generally, in her many pairs of beautiful shoes. She was the more glamorous of the two friends, the one who always wore makeup and took care of her appearance. It was a habit since she worked in the tourist office in Kilkenny and had to look smart for work.

Alice, on the other hand, had become used to working around the farm and the house, except for her part-time job at the hospital, when she wore a uniform. She and Tom seldom went out as a couple, except to the local pub, and that was not exactly an occasion to glam up. She had accepted that Tom Connolly was not a social animal and this was how her life was going to be from now on.

As they made their way to the top of the hill, they just stood there and laughed at the steep walk down towards the harbour. They were amazed at the choice of places to eat and all the Irish-named bars, but the women had agreed to try some of the local food on their first night. They spotted a place called La Bodega and decide to go in.

It looked different and interesting. There were just two tables available, and they took the one at the back by the wall. Their waiter came straight away with the menu, introduced himself as Danni, and offered to assist them if they had any difficulty deciding what to order.

As he walked away, Ruth, nudged Alice. "What about that? Is he good-looking or what?" They laughed out loud as they began to study the menu.

"How about the paella?" said Alice.

"I am feeling a bit adventurous", Ruth agreed, and Danni was back? Alice noticed the way he was looking at her friend and he didn't seem to see her sitting closest to where he was standing. She smiled to herself and had a look at Ruth, who was enjoying the attention. Of course, they ordered a bottle of wine, and Danni assured them that he would pick the perfect bottle for them.

The paella was perfect and so was the wine, and the service—they had never seen a waiter so conscientious. Did he pay so much attention to all the customers? Alice wondered if the restaurant employed waiters based on their looks. There were three of them there, one better-looking than the other, and Danni, even older than the others, was the most handsome. They would have to come here again.

Most of the other customers had gone when he came and sat at the table next to them. "Well, ladies, how was your food?" he asked.

"Very good", answered Ruth, turning briefly to Alice.

"And you, madam?"

"Yes, very nice indeed, thank you," she said, but Danni had already turned his attention back to her friend.

"Where are you from? When did you get here? Where are you staying?" It was a two-way conversation, and Alice just listened and watched the interaction between them until it was time to leave.

Ruth was the first to speak as they left and began to go further downhill. "What a lovely chap. You wouldn't get that sort of service at home".

Alice linked arms with Ruth. "So you think that was good service, do you?" They looked at each other. "He was flirting with you, woman", said Alice as she threw her head back and laughed, "and you told him everything he wanted to know. I thought you were going to give him your bank details." Alice sat on one of the many seats along the street and laughed heartily until Ruth finally saw the funny side of it. Then she felt a bit silly. Danni Garcia was the typical Spanish waiter, and she had been taken in by him.

Now it was time to check out some of the Irish pubs. One thing they had learned from the many holidays they had had with their husbands was that Irish bars are different to all the others. People go there to meet people and listen to music. They found a place with outside seating and decided to try it out. It was a real treat to sit outdoors in October and sip a glass of wine. Ruth was still thinking about the waiter, his accent, his dark brown eyes, his long perfect nose. Every detail was in her head, and she was hoping to see him again soon

Meanwhile, Alice was chatting to a woman at the next table and unaware of how unusually quiet her friend was, which was just as well. It was the oldest cliché in the book, foolish women falling for the waiter when they go on holiday.

Ruth had to try to join the company, bring her thoughts back to the moment, and get on with enjoying the first night of their holiday. The couple at the next table were from Cork and had also just arrived today. They were regular visitors to Lanzarote and knew all the best and cheapest places to go. They also suggested tours and places of interest and where to book these. A glass or two later they were laughing and joking and the music was starting inside. Ruth noticed that Alice was tapping her feet to the music, and it wasn't long before she took to the floor with the woman from Cork, whose name she found out later was Karen Brown, and her husband, Len.

Len reminded Ruth of Alice's husband, Tom Connolly. He was happy to sit there and have his drink and tell a joke or two, but she couldn't imagine him dancing.

Left to its own devices Ruth's mind returned to Danni. No man had ever looked at her like that, in a very long time. She was sure that he heard every word she said, and she wondered if he was married. "Don't be silly", she told herself. "Of course he is married. Men like him are not single. He probably has five children. The Spanish are like the Irish; they have large families." Then it came to her: "Maybe he is gay. Yeah, that's it". While all this stuff was going on in her mind, Ruth didn't notice how much she was drinking.

She was nearing the end of her third glass since they had gotten to the bar, was feeling a bit tipsy now, and did not even notice that Len had ordered another round for all four of them. Alice and Karen came and sat down to take a short break from dancing. It was obvious that they were having a great time.

Alice nudged her friend, "Go easy, you, or I'll have to carry you home. Come and join us for a dance. You are usually first on the floor". It was true, normally she would want to dance as soon as the music started.

"I must be tired from the journey and the early start", but it didn't seem right to talk about going back to the hotel when Alice was having such a good time. So she joined in and even enjoyed herself for a short while.

It turned out that the Browns were staying in the same area as the girls. This gave Ruth an idea, and she asked them if Alice could walk home with them, as she was tired and wanted to go back to the hotel. Alice was happy to stay on and dance the night away while Ruth took a taxi to their hotel.

As she entered the huge foyer, there was a sign for The Cactus Bar, Ruth took a stroll in that direction and found a large entertainment bar and a family show going on. She took a seat at the back and had a look. A waiter came, and she ordered a soft drink. It was nice to sit back and watch. It was too early to go to bed, and Alice was happy. Ruth was free to do what she wanted, a long way from home, away from everyone who knew her. It was a nice feeling.

That didn't last long. Suddenly, there he was, Danni Garcia, standing by her table. "May I sit down?"

Ruth didn't know what to say. "How did you know where to find me?"

"Do you work here?" He didn't wait for permission to sit down. "You told me where you were staying."

Ruth's mind was in turmoil. "Is he stalking me? Why did I come in here on my own? How will I get away?"

"I had to see you again. Please don't be alarmed; I don't run around after lady tourists. I was on my way home, thinking about you, so I decided to come in, hoping that you might be here. I'm glad now that I did. Where is your friend? Will you come to the restaurant again, or perhaps we could meet for a drink?"

"Hold on", said Ruth.

Danni prompted, "Okay".

"Danni, I can't go out with you; I have a husband at home. I don't go out with other men, and I'm sure you have a wife or something", she added.

"No, I don't. I am divorced and I have a daughter. She is seventeen."

The waiter was at the table. "Good evening, Signor Garcia." The two men shook hands by way of greeting.

"Hola, Pedro", said Danni then he ordered a beer and a glass of wine for Ruth, the same one she had with dinner.

If she had gone to her room, she would be tucked up in bed thinking about him, but this was very different and scary. Here he was sitting beside her, buying her a drink, and he was known here, which made her feel a bit more at ease.

He was looking at her intently as if he had never seen a woman before. Dennis had never looked at her like that in all the time she had known him. Dennis! Oh my God, she had forgotten to ring him as she had promised to do. With that Ruth stood up. "Sorry", she said, "but I must go. I must phone my husband".

Danni reached out and caught her hand. "I need to see you again, Siniora Ruth." He was holding her hand with both of his, and she felt the warmth of him.

She wanted to say yes but couldn't. He took her phone from her hand and put his number into it. He was standing so close now that she had to tilt her head back to look up at him. "I will put it under DG for Danni Garcia, and I will phone you tomorrow, okay?" Ruth nodded, and he bent down and kissed her full on the lips. It was more than a goodnight kiss. It was lingering and passionate and beautiful. He turned and walked out of the bar, but Ruth had to sit back down at the table and take a deep breath and some wine to steady herself. This certainly was a new experience and more than a bit disturbing. Ruth had not been kissed like that in a very long time and had forgotten what it felt like.

Chapter 3

When she arrived back at the apartment, Alice still had not returned. Should she ring her and find out if she was okay? Ruth had lost track of time, and it was only ten thirty. The kettle was just boiling when Alice appeared, tired from dancing, and with the early start that morning, she went straight to bed. After a quick cup of tea, Ruth followed her, but unlike her friend, she could not sleep. The image of Danni's face so close to hers and the memory of his kiss would never leave her.

Dennis had dropped her off at the train station this morning, but now it seemed like a lifetime ago. The familiar sound of her phone woke both; the sun was shining through the tiny opening in the blackout curtains. Reaching into her bag, which was on the floor beside her bed. It was a message from DG. "Can I see you tonight? Perhaps you will not come to my place, but I will look out for you. X."

"What is he talking about?" Ruth thought. "Oh my God, is he coming to our hotel again tonight? What is she getting into?

After the text from DG her phone rang. Alice sat up half asleep and said, "Whom the hell is ringing at this hour in the morning?" It was her husband Dennis.

Ruth answered. "How are you? Sorry I didn't ring you last night. We were so tired. What time is it now? Half nine? Half nine", she echoed for Alice's benefit.

Alice laughed and shouted, "Hello, Dennis", as she left the room.

Having filled her husband in on most of the details of the previous day, it was time for the first cup of tea on the balcony. Alice was down to her undies, taking in the rays, when Ruth came out to join her. "I could just sit here all day", said Alice.

"There is nothing to stop you from doing that. You are on holiday, remember?"

"I know", said Alice, "but I would feel lazy if I did nothing at all."

"Well, we could go to the beach and do nothing there", quipped Ruth, "and then you would feel like you did something".

The two women laughed. "Or we could go to the pool and still do nothing." The conversation continued in this vein until they were both hysterical. Yes, this was just what they needed, a good laugh.

"Did you walk home alone last night?" asked Alice.

"No, I got a taxi. It's not that far, but I didn't want to do it on my own."

"Yes, good idea", said Alice. "I did walk, with Karen and Len."

"Did you plan to meet them again? No plan, but I suppose we will bump into them. They are nice people, and Ned's Bar is their local when they are here. It is a nice bar, if you remember, owned by a man from Galway."

"Okay, let's try it again, then. There are so many places down there at the harbour it is a bit like being in Kilkenny, and I'm sure we will find more in the new town when we get around to it. We don't want to spend all our time with Irish people, do we? It's not like being with the men. We will have to go to some fancy places, while we have the chance. Let's find some brochures", said Ruth, "and try new things. How about we have dinner in the restaurant here tonight? I have heard that it is very good".

"Perfect", said Alice. "That's enough decision-making for today. I am going for a swim."

Ruth was going to just sit there and enjoy the warm sun but realised that she was more likely to think about the man she met last night, so she went to the beautiful pool and joined in some fun with other residents.

That evening, as they were getting ready to go to dinner, Ruth asked Alice if she had heard from Tom. Alice looked at her and smiled. "You know Tom, he will ring me if he needs anything, so no news is good news. It has been a long time since he phoned just to know how I am. I could run away with another man, and he wouldn't know that I was gone until he ran out of food or clean clothes."

"Surely", said Ruth, "that must piss you off".

"It probably would, if I thought too much about it, but I don't. There is no changing Tom Connolly now. His life is full of the farm and sport, and that's all he ever talks about. I am lucky to have you and my job."

Ruth thought about Dennis as she put the finishing touches to her makeup. At least they still talked to each other and went out the odd time. As for sex, that was almost a thing of the past. Then she remembered the kiss again and thought about telling Alice, but changed her mind. She knew Alice very well. Just the same, she didn't know what she would think about such a thing. *The* thing—a married woman kissing the first waiter she met. It was like her first kiss, and she wanted more. Of course, there was a feeling of guilt also, even though he kissed her and she did not return it, but she wanted to.

"You ready?" called Alice.

"On my way. Wow", said Ruth as she entered the lounge. "You look great tonight. I've never seen that on you before."

"Well, you don't usually see me ready to go out, and I do like that Galway man. You look very well yourself."

They laughed as they went up in the lift to the restaurant. It was a buffet meal, and everything looked beautiful.

The room was almost full, but they got a good table by the window, overlooking the pool.

"I could get used to this", said Alice as she raised her glass of wine. "It is good not to have to listen and agree with the men when you feel like hitting them. Sorry, Ruth. No, you are right, maybe I am better at hiding it." More laughter.

They had almost finished eating when Karen Brown came to their table. Good evening, ladies. How are you both, and did you have a good day?" They looked up and smiled at Karen, who didn't wait for their answer, just went on to tell them that they might see them later and gave them the name of the bar that they were going to, and then she was gone.

The two women were left looking at each other as if to say, "What happened there?" Each understanding the other, they smiled and finished their meal. As they were about to stand up, Ruth's phone sounded a text. Thinking that it was Dennis, she opened it, but it read, "DG."

Alice saw the shock on her friend's face. Who is it?" asked Alice.

"Just my sister-in-law. I will text her later."

"Okay, let's go for that walk. And let dinner settle before we meet the Browns and you start dancing."

Chapter 4

They strolled along the strip, stopping from time to time to admire something in a shop. Finally, Ruth got the chance she was waiting for. Alice went in to have a better look at a handbag. The phone came out and she could see what DG had to say. It read, "I hope to see you".

When Alice came back out, having bought the bag, Ruth said, "Come on, let's have a drink". She headed for the first bar that she saw and sat down. It was on the street, but that didn't matter. Ruth needed a glass of wine and Alice was delighted with her purchase.

Ruth was surprised when Alice suggested that they go to Ned's Bar, but she didn't care as long as she was not going to The Bodega. They got into a taxi and went to the harbour. It was a beautiful night, and they decided to sit outside on the veranda, where the seats were nice and comfortable. A young man came and took their order, and when he got back with their drinks, he informed them that they were paid for. Alice didn't seem surprised at all. Ruth looked at her. "Len and Karen, is it?"

"I don't think so", answered Alice coolly. It wasn't long before the person came to the table, a man about their age, fresh-looking and tanned, well dressed in light-coloured pants and a striped shirt. He was heavyset and had large hands and a great smile.

"Good evening, ladies", he said as he stood before them, then sat beside Alice. "I hope you had a nice day."

"Hello, Michael", said Alice. "This is my friend Ruth. Ruth, Michael Wall."

"My friends call me Mike", he replied.

They shook hands, and as Mike took Ruth's hand, that's when it dawned on her: "So that's why we are here and Alice made that special effort with her appearance, to meet Mike".

"I'm delighted ye came down", he said, looking directly at Alice. "I missed you last night, Ruth. Did you have an early night?"

"Yes, I was worn out, so I took myself home", Ruth said, feeling a bit guilty.

"Alice and I had a few dances and a bit of fun", Mike told her.

"Oh", said Ruth, nudging her friend and laughing, "you had fun, did you? You must have forgotten to tell me that, Mrs Connolly".

Alice laughed back and said, "I don't have to tell you everything, do I?"

With that, Alice nudged Ruth. "Look at who just arrived." It was Danni. "Isn't that your waiter from last night?"

He didn't hesitate to come straight to their table. He shook hands with Mike, said good evening, and then turned to the women. "The beautiful ladies from Ireland, it is good to see you back at this end of town. Do you mind if I join you, please?"

Mike pointed to the spare seat, and Danni sat down next to Ruth. "Please do, Danni. I can't keep them all to myself", Mike said, laughing. He went to introduce the girls, but Danni cut in.

"Yes, I know them."

They had another drink, then another. Mike told a few jokes, and Ruth tried to explain some of it to Danni, because even though his English was very good, some of it went over his head. Alice excused herself and went to the bathroom, and there was a moment's silence before Mike leaned toward Ruth.

"What a lovely woman your friend is. Do you think it would be OK to ask her to have dinner with me while you are here?"

Ruth was shocked. "Why are you asking me?"

He was almost whispering, "Maybe if you approved, she might say yes".

Ruth didn't want to encourage him. "It has nothing to do with me, Mike; Alice is a grown woman and can do as she pleases. You do know that she is married?"

"Yes, I do. It's entirely up to her then."

"Good God", thought Ruth, "we are sitting here like two couples. It is only our second day on the island and we have picked up two men". She laughed out loud, and the others wondered what was wrong with her. "Oh, it was just something I saw over there", she lied.

Alice came back and sat beside Mike Wall, as if it was the most natural thing in the world. He leaned close to her and asked if she was okay, like a loving husband might do.

Chapter 5

By the end of the night, Alice and Mike had danced several times, and they danced so well together, as if they had been doing it for years. And Danni had left, , without making plans to see Ruth again.

"He makes me feel so good, said Alice, like a woman. Sure, he is no oil painting, but he is very attractive. I haven't felt like that for a very long time, and I am only fifty-five after all. Would you mind if I left you alone one evening, Ruth? Mike has asked me to dinner, and of course, I know that I can rely on your discretion when we go home, not that Tom would care anyway, but you know how it is."

"Don't worry about me", said Ruth. "I will be happy to wander around. Sounds like you have made your decision, and don't worry, I won't say a word. Go and enjoy yourself, not as if you are doing anything wrong. It is just a bit of harmless flirting, and if it is more, it's none of my business. Good night, Alice."

"Night, hun", answered Alice.

Ruth didn't spend time worrying about what her friend was getting into. Instead, she thought about Danni. Would she meet him tomorrow? She drifted off to sleep without a thought for Dennis or her home.

The next day was spent at the beach, walking on the warm sand and swimming in the beautiful clear water. They paid a few euro on two sunbeds for the day, so that they could come and go to their apartment and not have to find a spare one every time.

Alice asked Ruth to rub on some sun oil, as she wanted a tan for tonight. She felt like a teenager going on a first date, with just a hint of guilt, which added to the excitement. "But what will you do for the night?" she asked.

"Look, Alice, don't you worry about me. I like the idea of being in a strange place on my own. I'll be like Shirley Valentine. You remember in the film where she ran away from home because she was tired of talking to the wall?"

They were bent over with laughter. "A bit like us", said Ruth, but she didn't mention Danni Garcia or the fact that she was hoping that he might ask her out tonight. He could even call to see her—unless she was completely mistaken and taken in by the first waiter who chatted her up.

Alice did think about Tom at home. She could guess what he was doing by the clock. He had a routine and never strayed from that. He would never think for one moment that she might be going out to dinner with another man, or even that a man might ask her out. That was the last time she thought about him that day.

She couldn't wait to start getting ready to go out, taking extra care about every part of it: body lotion, perfume, her hair, make-up, and all the details that other women do all the time. It had been a long time since Alice felt the need to look her best.

When she walked out of the bedroom, Ruth was gobsmacked. "Mrs Connolly, you look amazing."

"Thank you, my friend, I do feel it."

"Where are you meeting Mike?"

"I am taking a taxi to his bar, and we go on to who knows where from there."

Ruth hugged her and said, "You have a lovely evening, you deserve it".

Chapter 6

With Alice gone, Ruth opened a bottle of wine and went to sit on the terrace, still in her swimwear. Now, what to do, in Puerto Del Carmen, on her own. "This", she thought, "is what freedom feels like". But now that she had it, she didn't know what to do with it. Perhaps pull on some casual clothes and hit the shops for some bits and bobs to take home, or just sit here and do nothing. Then she got a text. It was from DG. It read, "Hola, Ruth, are you out tonight?" She sat there looking at it for what seemed like ages. What should she say? Would she tell him the truth, that she was there hoping he would call her, or do the sensible thing and lie, that she was out with her friend?

"I am at the hotel, thinking of going shopping." She pressed Send. A shiver went down her back. She was asking for trouble.

A quick shower and some make-up, and then call Dennis to ease her conscience. She wore her orange dress, best to show off her newly acquired tan, and they met in The Cactus Bar. Danni was sitting there at the counter when she went in. He looked so handsome, in a white shirt and jeans. The shirt showed off his colour and his broad back and shoulders. It was difficult to believe that he was there waiting for her. He got off the seat as she approached, and as he held both her hands, he kissed her on both cheeks, as is the custom in Spain. "Do you like to sit at the bar or a table, Ruth?"

"The bar is fine for me. Thank you."

He ordered two drinks, in Spanish, of course. Ruth thought how strange it was to be in the company of people whose language she could not understand. God knows what they were saying about her.

When their drinks arrived, Danni turned to face Ruth, and she was very aware of his legs almost touching hers. "You look beautiful tonight, as usual", he added. "Where is your friend?"

"Oh! She is out with an old friend", lied Ruth.

"So I have you all to myself." He laughed.

"No you don't", she snapped.

He caught her hand and smiled, showing off his perfectly white teeth. "Only joking. So, tell me all about yourself, what you do at home in Ireland."

"I am not sure what I should tell you, Danni. I barely know you, and we will never meet again after next week, or maybe even tonight."

He straightened his head and put on mock disappointment. "So you give me no hope at all", and he laughed.

Ruth laughed with him. "That's right. No hope for a man living in Lanzarote and a married woman living in Ireland. Now it was Ruth's turn. "So, tell me about you, Danni Garcia. Surely you have a beautiful Spanish lady at home."

He looked serious for the first time. "I am recently divorced, I told you. I loved her very much, but she left me and left the island. It was very final and painful for me. After that, I say to myself, 'That's it, no more love for me'. Then you come along."

She wanted to reach out and catch his hand but didn't. This was a time to be careful. Perhaps it was time to go back to the apartment, while she was still thinking straight. Instead, she joked, "When I go home, another woman will come along".

Danni turned away toward the bar, and Ruth couldn't see his face. She sipped her wine and waited for him to laugh. He didn't.

When he looked at her again, it was with a serious expression. It took what seemed like a long time for him to say, "You just put me in a packet, sorry, a box. You think I am like all Spanish men who wait on your table. Like all Irish people drink too much and curse a lot. Is that what you think, Ruth?"

"Oh, I am sorry. I was just trying to keep the mood light. I never meant to insult you, really, I didn't. Forgive me. Look, Danni, I am enjoying your company, that's all. Perhaps it is time to say goodnight."

Ruth slid off the seat, but he caught her by the hand before she had time to get away. "Please don't go. I want to spend time with you. You can laugh with your friends when you go home about the waiter who fell for you." He was smiling now, but there was something forced about it, and because she didn't want to go, she got back on the stool and continued to sip the wine.

Danni told her about how he came from Cordoba to live in Lanzarote, met his wife Carmen, and they had their daughter here. For what seemed like a long time, he talked and she listened. Yes, she was interested in his life, but mostly she liked looking at him. Suppressing the urge to reach out and touch him, Ruth knew that the wine was going to her head. They both spoke at the same time. He wanted to know all about her, and she suggested that they go for a walk. "Okay", Danni was quick to agree that a walk was a good idea.

They left the bar and began to walk towards the new town. The street lights were on, and the strip was thronged with holiday makers, just out for a stroll in the evening heat. There was a beautiful warm breeze. Ruth Cullen wasn't sure if it was the wine, the man beside her, or the atmosphere, but she felt young and carefree.

Chapter 7

Mike picked a restaurant within walking distance from his bar, right down at the harbour. He was well known there, and they were given the best table on the terrace, with a view of the Atlantic Ocean and all the boats moored there, just moving gently. It was very beautiful. Mike asked if Alice liked fish and said that this was one of the best places in the town to get all sorts of fish. He went through the menu and told her about each dish she was interested in. He knew how each one was cooked and any sauce that came with it.

Alice couldn't help but compare him to Tom, who would expect her to know such things, even though she had never been there before. Mike picked the wine and topped up her glass regularly.

He was keen to know about his dinner guest and her life in Kilkenny. He had also come from a farming family in Galway. He would have liked to be the one to farm the land, but his brother inherited the farm and the family home, so he was given money, and he headed to the sun. He had no regrets and went home regularly to visit. They had lots to talk about and were very relaxed in each other's company. Alice thought that he might have been just like Tom, had he stayed in Galway. But right now, she was glad that he was here and she was being wined and dined (a phrase women love to use when they are dreaming) by a lovely man.

The owner came to their table to ask if they were enjoying their food. Mike introduced Alice to him. His name was Juan. He asked if she was from Ireland, and she said, "Yes, and I love your food. I will come back here again soon with my friend".

"Yes, please do, and your wine will be on me, as you are a friend of Mike. He is a good man." The two men shook hands, and Juan left them to finish their coffee. Alice took notice of the name over the restaurant, Puerto Bahia, and the blue-and-white nautical theme. Yes, she would take Ruth here tomorrow to make up for leaving her on her own tonight.

They left the harbour and walked slowly uphill. Mike pointed out different things of interest to Alice, things that she would never have seen had he not been with her. He steered her through the crowds that gathered here and there and caught her hand to cross the street. Her instinct was to pull her hand away, but instead, she felt the warmth of his hand holding hers, and it made her feel like he really cared about her.

For the first time, Alice Connolly felt that she was out with a man, and she looked at Mike as if seeing him for the first time. She looked at his round, happy face, and he was looking back at her. He let her hand go. "Sorry, Alice. I shouldn't have done that." They continued to walk in silence; their friendship had changed.

Before they got to the hotel, Mike asked if she would like to stop for a drink.

"Yes, good idea." A young lady took their order, and they looked at each other. Alice took the lead. "It has been a lovely night, thank you, but we can't do it again." She reached across the table and touched his hand.

Their drinks arrived, and Mike picked up his glass and looked into it and without looking at Alice and simply said, "Why?"

"What do you mean?"

"I mean why can't we enjoy another night out? We are not doing any harm to anyone."

"Mike, I know just one way to say this, so I am going to be straight with you: When you caught my hand tonight, I felt something, a feeling I have not had for a very long time."

"Yes", answered Mike, "I know the feeling very well. I felt it the first time I set eyes on you".

Alice was a bit angry now. "And you say we are doing no harm. Well, we are, Mike, to each other."

"Alice, time is precious, and we don't meet people we are so attracted to every day, so please, let's enjoy spending a few hours together while we can. I don't mind if Ruth is with us. I know you can't leave her alone."

Alice thought this was so nice, and she wanted to kiss him for being so thoughtful. She had forgotten that not all men were like Tom, and had come to expect very little from them.

Chapter 8

Danni and Ruth walked for a while, met a few people he knew, and stopped to greet them. Ruth was getting used to all the hugging and kissing and how Spanish people interacted, until they reached a cocktail bar that looked very inviting.

"Would you like a cocktail, Ruth?"

"Okay, why not? It's not every day one feels this sort of freedom."

Danni pulled out a chair for her, and she picked up a menu. Instead of sitting at the other side of the round table, he sat close to her. She was pretending not to notice, when he caught her hand and looked straight into her face. "What would you like? Perhaps sex on the beach." He laughed. She could feel his eyes on her, and she knew that he was waiting for a reaction.

"No", said Ruth calmly. "I will have a Long Island iced tea, thank you." A waiter came to the table, and he ordered two iced teas.

They never had cocktails when on holiday with their husbands; Tom Connolly said that they were too fancy and too expensive. "Well, maybe they are for him", thought Ruth, "but not for me. Tonight, I am having fun with a Spanish waiter". The bar was full inside and out, and it felt good to just sit there sipping her drink and watching the people go by.

It was Danni who broke the silence between them. "Ruth, I could sit here all night and look at you." His face was so serious.

"Stop it, Danni. Let's just enjoy ourselves."

"I am enjoying myself", he answered, and I want you to enjoy it too. "Will you come to see my house? I live close by and would love for you to visit." She didn't run away like she should have, if she had not been drinking. She just sat there looking at him, wanting to lean over and kiss him.

As they walked up a side street, his arm around her, he stopped, turned to face her, and kissed her, gently. Ruth felt pure sexual desire and couldn't wait to get to his apartment. He opened the front door and stood back to allow her in, but she stopped in front of him in the doorway and put her arms around his neck, her body pressed against his. She was in no doubt that he felt the same. Danni kicked the door shut and steered her to his bedroom. He undressed her slowly and carefully, as if their lives depended on it, driving Ruth crazy with longing to get her hands on him. Ruth didn't know that she could want sex so much. When they were both naked and he bent down to kiss her breasts, Ruth leaned back until she was on the bed. Danni followed her lead, knowing exactly what she wanted and understanding her urgency. All doubts and guilt were gone. They were two people desperate for each other, and she had never had sex like this before, never wanted a man so much, and absolutely didn't expect to have so much appetite for sex. She wanted it to go on forever and had no inhibitions whatsoever.

When they walked back to her apartment, it was almost 2:00 a.m. What would she tell Alice? Who could she say she was with? Suddenly it was like being late home from school. That sex-starved woman was replaced with a frightened girl. "I suppose", she said to Danni, "I could tell her where I was and with whom".

"Yes", he answered. "You are a free woman, not a slave." He turned her round to face him and kissed her again. "A very beautiful woman."

When they reached the main entrance of the hotel. Ruth stopped. "Okay, this is as far as you can go." He wrapped his arms around her and held her so close, she knew that he did not want the night to end, but she had no choice.

She turned the key in the door gently, hoping to get in without Alice noticing her. Thank God she was gone to bed. Ruth sat down and began to think about the night she had had. This needed a cup of tea. She put the kettle on and went to the bedroom to put on her night clothes. Alice was not in her bed, and a wave of panic hit Ruth. Where was she?

There was only one thing for it: ring her. "If I don't get an answer, I will have to contact the police." Totally panicked now, she got her phone. There were four missed calls and one new message. It was Alice, and the message was four hours old. "Ruth, don't worry, I will not be home. I will see you tomorrow." The kettle was boiling, and she made a cup of tea and sat at the table. "Alice, what are you doing, staying out all night with a man?" This was a shock; Alice Connolly was having an affair. She thought of Tom and laughed. Who could blame her? Her own dalliance was forgotten now; it was time for sleep.

Chapter 9

Another beautiful sunny day in Lanzarote, and Ruth decided to go to the dining room for a full breakfast. She left a note for Alice to join her there. Halfway through breakfast, Alice arrived. She had been to the apartment and changed her clothes. "Good morning", said Ruth cheerfully.

"And a very good morning to you, too, Mrs Cullen", said Alice, equally cheerful. Alice had had breakfast, but she sat there until her friend had finished. They went back to their apartment to discuss the night before.

"Go on, then. Tell all, you dirty stop-out-all-night." They laughed. Alice sat down at the balcony table and began to tell her friend about the night out with Mike Wall, about the lovely night they had and how they went to his apartment, sat down to watch TV, and fell asleep. Mike was sitting in the corner of the sofa, and she lay back against his chest, her legs on the sofa, and he put both arms around her.

Alice was bubbling over with excitement. "Honestly, Ruth, it was amazing. We were so comfortable together.

I knew that I was falling asleep but didn't want to get up from there, and his arms were still around me when I did wake at six this morning. I stood up then, straight away, before I made a fool of myself and began to rip the clothes off him."

"I doubt that he would have pushed you away", laughed Ruth. "I know said Alice, but there is a big difference between liking his company and going all the way".

Now Ruth knew that she could not talk about her night of passion with Danni. Yes, it was beautiful, but not in the same way that the other woman had described her night. Anyway, how could you tell anyone the intimate details of such an experience? She doubted that her friend had ever had sex like that in her life, just as she had not.

"So do you and Mike have plans to meet today?"

"No plans, he will ring me later. What do you want to do today?"

"I think I will have a lie down. I did a long walk last night and had a few drinks along the way." What she really wanted to was lie in bed and remember every detail of her time in Danni's bed and hope that he would text her and maybe they could do it all again. She didn't dare think of her husband, because it had nothing to do with him or her life at home. This was just sex, nothing more. She had often heard of people having holiday romances, but now she was having one, and it had to remain a secret.

Alice, on the other hand, was having a friendship with Mike. Mind you, if that had happened at home, tongues would be wagging, but it was different here. Everyone was on holiday, and Alice and Mike could be just any middle-aged couple having a night out. What about herself and Danni? The very thought of him brought back the memories of last night, their bodies entangled, the orgasm that blew her mind. About that time, she fell asleep and didn't wake again until Alice came to ask if she wanted to go out for lunch.

While eating their pizza, the girls decided it was time to take a tour around the island. On the way back they went to visit one of the many tour operators and took some brochures to help them to see what was available. As they were paying the bill, Alice got a phone call from Mike. Ruth left a tip and walked away, to give them some privacy. She was sitting on a stone wall when her friend caught up with her. Alice was excited as she explained that Mike would drive them around to all the sights on the island. "It will be great. We can stop when we want to and get the best food, outside of Puerto Del Carmen."

"That sounds good", said Ruth. "When will we go?"

"Tomorrow, if that is okay with you."

"Perfect, it's about time we did some tourist stuff. Now let's hit the pool for the afternoon. We must have something to show off when we get home."

Lying at the pool was bliss, with the warmth of the sun and the sound of children playing in the water. Ruth was dozing when she heard her phone ringing. It was Dennis. He was just checking to see if they were enjoying themselves. "Yes, it is fabulous, Dennis. We are at the pool now soaking up the rays, and tomorrow we are going on a tour of the island."

"Lovely, how is Alice?"

"Here beside me sleeping."

"Make sure that she has plenty of cream on her, and you do the same."

"Ok, hun. Talk to you soon."

Chapter 10

Mike arrived to collect them the next morning early. He was driving a jeep. It was a safari type, the best way to see the island. "Ladies, you must forget the hairstyles while we are in this." Mike laughed heartily.

This was a real treat, and the two women giggled. "Who needs a bus?" Alice took the front seat, and Ruth saw how the driver looked at her. She could swear it was love in that look. It didn't take long to get out of town and on to the main road. The traffic was moving fast, and Ruth barely heard her phone. It was a text from Alice's sister, Sarah, who worked with Ruth. It read, "Please ring me when my sister is not listening. There is something I must tell you",

The scenery was amazing and different, and Mike stopped from time to time to explain about the volcanic landscape, so Ruth didn't have much time to think about the text until they stopped for lunch.

When she got the opportunity, she did ring Sarah. "Oh, Ruth I am glad that you rang. It's Tom. He has had a heart attack."

"Oh my God", said Ruth. "Is he okay?"

"I don't know. He is in hospital, and they are not telling us much. The girls are home and are there waiting for news."

"I will have to tell her, won't I?"

"I am not sure, Ruth. Should we wait a few hours to see if it is serious? It's not as if she can come home tonight."

"Yes, you're right. Sarah, will you check flights and see when she can get home?"

"Okay," said Sarah, and she rang off.

Ruth had to take time to get it together before joining the others. Alice and Mike were deep in conversation when Ruth joined them.

Alice looked at her friend. "Dennis?"

"Who else?" laughed Ruth. They carried on with the tour, but Ruth's heart wasn't in it. When it was time to go back, Mike announced that he was taking them both to the best place he knew for dinner. She waited until they got back to town to say that she was not in the mood for eating and suggested that they go on to dinner without her.

When she arrived at their hotel, Ruth went straight to the apartment and just sat there on the terrace. Should she have told her friend the truth. Tom might have been dying and, she had left Alice to go out with another man. However, if she had told her, they would both have to sit here and worry. What more could they do? She told herself that she had done the best thing for Alice. It could be her last night on the island, and she deserved to enjoy it.

Then she wondered what she should do if her friend was going home tomorrow. Should she go with her? Time to go upstairs and get a bottle of wine. She needed to relax and see what happened next.

Mike told Alice that they were going to El Golfo. It meant nothing to her, but she trusted him to take her to the right place. As they began the drive out of town, he explained that they were going north to a little village that served the best seafood on the island.

Fish was not her favourite food, but this evening she was prepared to try new things. He drove by the scenic route, showing her the villages along the way. The warm breeze was blowing her hair all over the place, but it didn't matter. Nothing mattered, only that she was with the nicest man she had ever met.

Alice was secretly delighted that her friend had opted out of the rest of the evening. She wanted to be alone with Mike. It was time to admit to herself that she fancied him and he was not just a friend anymore. When they reached their destination and parked right in front of the ocean, it was just a few steps to where they were going to eat. They were seated right by the water, and their waiter put them side by side so that they could both look out to sea.

They ordered their food and some drinks, and while waiting for it to arrive, Mike reached over and took Alice by the hand. He looked at her seriously and said, "I have something to ask you, and I want to say it before we have a drink". Alice held her breath.

"Will you stay with me tonight?" He kept talking, "Not like the last night? I want us to sleep together and wake up together in the morning. It has been a very long time since I felt like this about a woman, Alice, and we have so little time. I realise that it is not sensible for us to become involved, but I think we are that already". He looked at her for confirmation, and he got it loud and clear as Alice leaned over and kissed him passionately.

"Let's do it", she said, smiling from ear to ear.

Suddenly the food and the view were not so important.

Chapter 11

It was almost ten o'clock when Sarah finally phoned Ruth. Tom had a heart attack, but he was now stable, and they would know more in the morning. Meanwhile, Sarah had checked flights for her sister to come home. It was Saturday, and she could get a flight first thing in the morning. It was going to be very expensive, but after that, the next direct flight would be Tuesday.

Sarah asked to speak to her sister, but Ruth explained that she had gone out with friends they had met and had not been told about her husband's condition. Sarah sounded shocked. "Why didn't you tell her, Ruth?"

"There was no point in her sitting here worrying when she could do nothing about it", answered Ruth. "Is Tom being kept in the hospital?"

For a moment Sarah was quiet. "We don't know yet", she answered tersely. She clearly was not happy with Ruth.

"I will get her to ring you when she gets back, and you can fill her in."

Sarah hung up without saying goodbye. She could understand that Sarah was upset. Tom was her brother-in-law after all, but even if he had died, Alice could not do anything from here.

Ruth tried to ring her friend but got no answer. She could not even leave a message. In a bit of a panic now, what would she tell Sarah if she phoned again? There was nothing she could do about it. She poured another glass of wine and sat back. She could hear the Atlantic Ocean. The tide was in, and the sound of it lapping on the sand was so peaceful, it was hard to believe that there was a very busy street outside.

The sound of her phone broke the quietness. It was Sarah again.

"Hello! Hello! Hello!" This was all Ruth could think of. She wondered why she was not ringing her sister.

Sarah was talking to someone at the other end of the line: "She can't hear me. Try Alice again. Thank God your dad is okay, or we would have to contact the police". Ruth pressed the button and cut them off.

"So, Tom is out of danger." She was glad that she did not tell Alice. She knew how Alice and Tom's marriage worked, and her friend really needed this break away from him. Alice would not have said it like this. She had a sense of duty to her husband and never openly criticized him. Instead, she talked about their marriage as if it was totally normal. Ruth knew better. At least she and Dennis had similar interests and went out as a couple, even talked and laughed together sometimes

She tried to contact Alice, several more times before she went to bed. Danni phoned her, but she ignored him. It was more important to be here when Alice came home, and she knew that he would contact her again tomorrow. As she drifted off to sleep, she could hear her phone but decided not to answer it.

It was no surprise to find the second single bed empty again in the morning. Who would have thought that Alice Connolly would have a holiday romance? She was much more likely to be there complaining about the heat or the price of last night's dinner. What a strange situation. Just as Ruth boiled the kettle for her first cup of tea, the phone began to ring, Sarah, then Dennis. As she could not account for Alice, there was no point talking to either of them. Dennis had tried to ring her last night. That was the call she ignored before falling asleep. Of course, he would know about Tom being in hospital.

Chapter 12

Mike dared Alice to order something that she had never tasted before, but she was slow to take him up on that. It wasn't in her nature to be adventurous. However, tonight was different. She had said yes to sleeping with this lovely man, so she ordered a platter of seafood. It was almost all new to her, apart from a few prawns.

He had the same and talked her through each mouthful as she ate squid, octopus, scallops, and a few others that were new to her taste buds. Mike had ordered the perfect wine to accompany the fish. She would remember Costa Azul Restaurant forever. Mike promised to take her back to El Golfo again, to see the Green Lagoon. "We will take Ruth with us. It is very beautiful", he said. Alice noticed that he said "us" like they were a couple.

She thought about calling Ruth to let her know that she was not coming back, but there was no need. Ruth knew that she was with Mike and would not be worried.

They drove back to Puerto Del Carmen in relative silence, giving Alice time to think about what she was doing, but she thought more about what was going to happen than she did about what she should be doing. She and Tom had been married for twenty-four years, and she had never thought about having sex with another man, not even since they had stopped being any close and sharing a bed.

Mike's apartment was small compared to a normal house at home. Having said that, everything you could need was there, and the balcony was beautiful. It did not have a sea view like the hotel. Instead, it looked out to the rocky landscape and had a view of the golf course in the distance. They had complete privacy, so they sat out there with a glass of wine each.

Mike sat back in the small wicker cushioned sofa and sighed. Alice looked at him, wondering about the sigh. In answer, he took her hand, lifted it to his mouth, and kissed it. Looking into her eyes, he said, "It feels so good having you here, Alice, and knowing that you are not going to run back to your hotel is a real gift to me".

Alice leaned forward and kissed him on the mouth. She had wanted to do that all night. Her kiss was returned, and she could feel passion boiling up, but Mike let her go and sat back. "There is no hurry. Let us just enjoy the feeling for a while."

Alice laughed. "You are an awful man to keep a woman waiting like this."

He took her hand and asked, "When was the last time you felt like this, Alice?

Looking sadly out at the horizon, tears flowed down her face as she answered, "A very long time ago".

Mike held her hand against his face lovingly. "That is such a shame, to have a beautiful woman like you unloved and not desired the way I want you now."

"Women my age don't usually have or want sex, and when you have been married to the same man for over twenty years, that part of your life is over. He looked at her with a puzzled expression on his face. But you do want sex now, don't you, Alice?"

Without hesitation, she answered, "Yes, with you. He put his hand under her dress and let it rest on the inside of her knee. She put her head back and moaned, willing him to keep going. She put her hand to the back of his head and kissed him hard on the lips. When they stopped, she said, "Let's go to your bedroom. I want you now, Mike".

They made love twice before curling up together. Alice was surprised at his stamina, but she was more surprised at her own part in having sex with a man she hardly knew. She never remembered wanting a man so much or taking such an active part in the sex act. Her life with Tom Connally would never be the same again. She was not an old sexless woman, far from it. She lay awake remembering what they had done and enjoying the feeling of Mike's naked body beside her. So this was what had been missing from her life all these years.

They were going to have breakfast, but Alice felt a bit guilty about leaving Ruth on her own for so long and decided to go back to the apartment. It was almost lunchtime when Alice got back. She was glowing and obviously happy, almost like a different woman. Ruth got off the sun lounger and put the kettle on. What else would an Irish woman do before giving her best friend such news.

"Sorry to burst your bubble now, my friend, but I have something to tell you. Tom is in hospital."

Alice sank into the nearest chair. "Go on", she said, all the happiness draining from her face.

"Seems he had a heart attack."

"Oh shit", exclaimed Alice. "Is he okay?"

"Yes, I think so. Sarah was ringing me and you, so I stopped answering my phone. I could hardly tell them where you were, and anyway, I didn't know. You had better ring home, and remember, you had no signal until now."

She rang her sister. "Sarah, what has happened? Sorry, my battery ran out and I didn't think that anyone would be ringing me. Tell me about Tom. Is he still in the hospital? Was it a serious heart attack?" Then she stopped talking.

"Alice, you know that a heart attack is always serious, but he is stable now and out of danger. He will probably be left home later today." In almost the same sentence, she said, "When will you be home?"

"Is he being allowed to go home?"

"Yes, I think so", answered Sarah.

"Who is with him now?"

"Holly, she came straight away. But surely you want to be with your husband at this time."

"Well of course I do, but it is not easy to get a flight, and it will cost a fortune."

Alice could hear the irritation in her sister's voice: "Imagine how it looks, you God knows where on holiday and Tom having a heart attack".

"I know", said Alice, "but our daughter is with him and he is out of danger. Look, Sarah, I will ring the hospital and see if they think I need to come home. I have nine more days here. I must consider Ruth as well". Alice felt in charge now.

Sitting in the sun, she thought about her husband, in hospital, expecting her to run home and make a fuss over him. Then she thought of Mike and the wonderful night they just had together. Her sister worried about what the neighbours thought. What was she to do?

"Okay, Sarah, I will have a look at flights into all airports and see what I can do. In the meantime, keep me informed, Sis. Talk later, bye."

The last thing Alice wanted to do was go home, but she knew that it was the right thing to do and it was expected of her. Then she felt anger boil up inside her. Tom and his bloody heart attack. Why couldn't he wait until she was home? Hadn't she given him enough of her life? The first time she got away on her own, he must go and destroy it.

Chapter 13

Then she thought of Mike. Should she ring him? Would he care if she was going home, or not? He was just a holiday fling, after all, not as if they were in a relationship.

Ruth came and joined her friend. She put a comforting hand on her shoulder. "You okay, hun?"

"Yes", answered Alice in a barely audible voice. When Ruth was seated, she could see that Alice was crying.

"Go on", said Ruth, "tell me about last night. Did you have a good time?"

Wiping her eyes, she nodded. "The best night of my life." Then she laughed, looked at the other woman, and added, "And that includes my wedding night." Ruth reached out and took her hand, and they both laughed heartily. "I am so happy for you, Alice", said Ruth.

"But, what now? Do you want to go home?"

Alice shook her head, then answered, "I suppose I will have to, though, or I will never live it down. I might be able to claim from the insurance for the lost days and an urgent flight, seeing as it is my nearest and dearest". Another understanding laugh from both.

"Will you tell him that you must go home? Yes. I will book a flight first, then ring him. Little did I know when I woke up this morning that I would have to go home today. Will you be okay here on your own?"

"Yes, I will. I feel like I know the place well enough, and I don't have to go far to eat or go to the beach, and plenty of security here." Still no mention of Danni. "Do you need help with anything, Alice?"

"No thanks."

"I will go for a stroll, then, and let you get on with it? Ring me if you need anything." Ruth grabbed her bag and left her friend to pack her bags and prepare to go back to the man she barely liked, let alone loved. It seemed so unfair.

However, here Ruth was now, in beautiful Lanzarote for over a week on her own, free to do as she pleased. She could browse the shops all day if she wanted, or just lie by the pool and read. She was excited as she took in the sheer beauty of the sea, people swimming and having fun, small sailboats bobbing around, and a very large cruise ship on the horizon

What she did not see was the man striding towards her, until they were just a few meters from each other. He stopped just before she reached him, and Ruth saw Danni just before she bumped into him. He put both arms out, and she walked straight into them as they hugged warmly.

Immediately aware of his lean and strong body, Ruth didn't want to take her hands off him. Now the only beauty she could see was the man guiding her to a seat slightly along from where they met.

When they sat down, he looked intently at her and said, "I have missed you, Ruth. Why didn't you answer my calls?" Ruth told him about Alice and her husband and how she had to keep the phone free. It seemed like a lame excuse now that she had said it, and if he had said it to her, she doubted that she would be impressed.

As they sat there holding hands, Ruth became aware once more of why she was so attracted to this man, but wondered why he was so interested in her. She had been out with a few fellas before she met and married Dennis, but since then no man had shown an interest in her.

Now Danni Garcia had awakened a part of her that she couldn't deny. Now Ruth suddenly realised that with Alice gone home, she could have Danni come to her apartment.

Feeling guilty now for just thinking such a thing, she pulled her hand away from him and went to stand up, but he gently pulled her back to the sitting position and asked why she was leaving. "I need to go back to my friend and help her get ready to leave."

"Can I see you later, for dinner maybe?"

"Yes, that would be nice. I will come to your place. Is that okay?"

"Lovely." He kissed her hand and let her go.

Ruth was filled with excitement and some guilt as she walked back to the hotel. Poor Alice had to go home and miss out on the first holiday without Tom—home to wait on him hand and foot like she always had.

How did women get into that situation? Younger women don't do that anymore. They start as they mean to go on. They don't become slaves to their husbands, sorting out their every little problem. We may as well be their mothers who looked at men as people who needed to be cared for.

When she got back to the hotel, Mike was sitting on a seat outside. Ruth sat beside him. "She won't talk to me, Ruth. She says that it's over and I must forget her. It might be that easy for her, but not for me. I fell in love with Alice, and believe me, I don't do that every day. Will you ask her to see me, please, Ruth, even if it is to say goodbye? It's not over, Ruth. It can't be."

She could see that he was close to tears. She reached over and took his hand in sympathy, as she could not see any way that they might be able to meet again.

Chapter 14

On entering the room, Ruth could see Alice on the terrace. "Are you okay?" asked Ruth.

"Ya," was all she got back. She was not sure if she should tell her friend about the man outside waiting to see her.

"Any word from Tom?"

"Yes", said Alice. "He managed to phone me to know when I would be home. He forgot to ask if I was coming home. Ruth, I am so cross with him, I think I might hit him when I see him. The one time I manage to get away from him, now here I am running back. He can leave anytime he likes to go away with his GAA mates, without a thought for me."

"Mike is outside waiting for you, hoping to talk to you?"

"I know, but it will be easier if I don't see him again. I don't want to say goodbye to him."

"Then don't say goodbye. Just say, 'Until we meet again'. He is from Galway, after all, and nothing is stopping you from coming back here again."

Alice's face lit up at that. "You know what, Ruth, you are right. I will go out to see him."

Ruth poured herself a glass of wine and sat in the sun. "Who would have thought it? Alice Connolly falls in love on holiday. Of all the women in the world, she would have been the last one I would have expected that to happen to. I'm sure she will settle back into life on the farm when she gets back. After all, what choice does she have? You can't sell a farm and divide the spoils, and her part-time job at the hospital does not pay very much."

Her pondering was cut short when Alice and Mike came into the apartment, both smiling now. "I will take this lovely lady to the airport", said Mike to Ruth.

"Very nice. Make sure you have enough time, now. You don't want to be cuddling when the plane is taking off."

They all laughed, and Mike reached for Alice's hand. They look like a couple, thought Ruth.

Ruth went for a swim and then lay in the evening heat till it was time for dinner. She put in no special effort when getting ready, before she strolled along to Danni's workplace. As she was about to order, her phone rang. It was Dennis. They chatted as she pointed to what she wanted on the menu. "I wondered how you would feel being there on your own", he told her. she assured him that she was okay and would enjoy herself.

"Aren't you the independent one?" Dennis laughed.

"Yes, I am, I suppose. Poor Alice will be back to fetching and carrying again tomorrow. Have you heard anything of Tom? Is he okay?"

"Yes, he is, and from what I hear, he has no shortage of people to look after him."

"OH, what do you mean by that?"

"Never mind, I will tell you when I see you. Probably just gossip. You know what it is like around here."

"I must go now. Dinner has arrived."

"Okay. Enjoy. Talk soon."

She had almost finished her meal when Danni arrived and came straight to her table. "Do you mind if I sit down, Ruth?"

"Of course not, but are you supposed to be working?" He grinned. "No, only if it is busy, and as you can see, it is not."

Confused, Ruth asked, "And do you get paid for sitting here with me?"

"Yes, I pay myself for talking to you", he said, laughing. "This is my restaurant, Ruth, and I would talk to you even if I got no pay for doing it. How are you planning to spend the rest of your evening?"

"I have not decided yet", she said, leaving it open for him to suggest both.

"Cocktails in the sun, then, to start with. How does that sound?"

"That sounds great", answered Ruth.

The following morning, she lay in Danni's bed as if it was normal, and she remembered the sex they had just a few hours ago. She was amazed at how she could give her body to this man with complete abandon. She trusted him to find all the right spots to drive her crazy with desire. He was still sleeping now, and she hoped that when he woke up, they might do it again.

How had she gotten to this age and never experienced such pleasure in sex before? Even when they were first married, she and Dennis never had a relationship like this. It was a dull routine and gave her little or no pleasure, so she had come to believe that was how it was for everyone.

Danni Garcia stretched and put his arm around her, and her response was immediate. She turned to face him. There was no worry about morning breath, and he kissed her passionately. She put her leg around him, just to be closer, and before long they were as close as two people can be.

He was inside her, moving slowly, and Ruth had raised her arms to the headboard. She was in heaven as she looked at the beautiful stranger who was taking her there. She knew nothing about him and didn't need to. They continued to explore each other's bodies for another hour or so. Then Ruth wanted to be alone, to stroll along the street and think about her time with Danni.

He wanted to walk with her, but she declined. She was going back to her apartment. As she strolled along the crowded street in the warm breeze, she wondered if any of them had sex like she had this morning. She smiled to herself, thinking, "I bet they didn't".

Chapter 15

Mike stood in the queue with Alice while she waited to check her bag in, and only left her when she was next to go through. She wanted to turn back and go with him, but it was not an option. She was going home, and that was it.

It was Mike who said, "Okay, it is time for me to get out of here". They turned towards each other and hugged for what seemed like ages; neither wanted it to end. Then he walked away without saying another word.

The person behind the desk said, "Next please", and Alice approached, never looking back.

She would never forget the loneliness she felt as the plane began to taxi. This was it; she would never see Mike Wall again. There was no choice now but to concentrate on going home and what might lie ahead for her. The first surprise was her sister Sarah waiting at the airport, which was not part of the plan. Sarah hugged her and took her bag. "Why are you here?" asked Alice.

"I thought you might not want to do the train journey alone, and I need to take you straight to the hospital."

"The hospital! Why?"

"Tom is back in there. He was feeling bad, and Holly rang the ambulance."

"When did this happen? This morning early. He was feeling dizzy and not able to do his work, and you know that it would have to be bad to keep him from the farmyard."

"God, it must be bad."

When they reached the hospital, Alice was directed to the ward where her husband was. He was hooked up to some machines. Alice expected her daughter to be there, but instead, Ann Nolan was sitting there holding his hand. She knew that Ann was working with Tom in the GAA, but not that they were this close.

Alice just stood there watching, before Tom saw her and Ann let his hand go. She jumped out of the chair. "Oh, Alice, thank God you are back. This fella needs some TLC. He seems to be doing okay though, Alice."

Alice was not going to address Tom while Ann Nolan was there, so she just stood there and waited for her to go. She got the message and left, saying, "Hope to see you soon, Tom".

Alice sat down and asked, "What is going on with you?"

"I don't know, girl. They said that the first was just a mild heart attack and they would call me back later for tests, but I felt weak as a kitten this morning. Good thing Holly was there."

Alice felt guilty that she had no sympathy for her husband of over twenty years. She just sat there and asked him questions. "How long do you think they will keep you here? Is there anything you need?"

"No thanks, Ann picked up a bag for me this evening."

"I didn't know that you two were so close. Maybe I could have stayed in Lanzarote and asked Ann how you were doing."

"Now, Alice, there is no need for sarcasm. Ann is a friend, and you are my wife, and I need you to be here."

Later that night, as she sat at home, it struck her how insistent her sister had been that she got home straight away, to the point of collecting her from the airport and going straight to the hospital. Did she know that Ann Nolan would be there? Was that why Sarah had stayed outside? "Anyway", thought Alice, "who cares?" As she climbed into bed, all she could think of was Mike. She ached for him, to be with her, to hold her hand, to put his arm around her, and to curl up beside him in his bed.

Chapter 16

Ruth felt like a young woman as she donned her best bikini and headed for the pool. The sun loungers were leather and comfortable, and she lay down her towel and stretched out in the warm sunshine. She thought of her friend back in Ireland, poor Alice. When she spoke to Dennis later, she had to remember to ask what he meant about Tom Connolly not being short of company. It was difficult to imagine any woman being interested in him.

Danni, on the other hand—she was surprised that he was not attached, and there was no sign of a woman in his apartment, just a few items belonging to his daughter, who was at school on the mainland. Perhaps he settled for numerous affairs like her.

Strangely enough, that didn't bother her. She was having the holiday romance that people always dreamed about. Then back to normal in a few days, it would be hard to get into the job and the routine again, but she would always have her dream and her secret. She was glad that Alice didn't know about Danni.

That evening Ruth decided to get into a pair of shorts and sandals, go for a good walk, and pick up a takeaway along the Avenida, which Danni had taught her to say. The beachside was good for walking, as it was cooler with the sea breeze and not so crowded with shoppers. This walk would make up for the time she lay dreaming by the pool all day. She didn't think about Dennis all day; this is what a holiday should be like.

However, this freedom of mind did not last long, when she heard Karen Brown calling her name as she approached them, coming from the opposite direction. "Hello, stranger", said Karen.

Len just nodded. "Ruth!"

"So where is Alice this evening?" She laughed. "Or have you fallen out?"

Without meaning to, Ruth spilt out the truth about Tom being in the hospital. As she was saying it, she knew it was a mistake.

"Oh, poor Alice, and did she have to go back alone? How awful for her. And tell me, how is he now?"

Thinking on her feet now, Ruth answered, "I will be talking to her later and get the full details".

She hadn't even thought about Alice all day, her mind too taken up with Danni Garcia and sex.

"Do you have dinner plans this evening?" asked Karen.

"No", replied Ruth. She knew what was coming next.

"Okay, you can join us. We are going to La Trattoria. You know the one opposite The Casino. We will meet you there in half an hour."

"Okay." It was not so much an invitation as an order.

That was the walk destroyed, all the serenity gone, replaced with how to get through the evening with the Browns, and of course, she should ring her friend to see how she was and find out about Tom. She also had to warn Danni not to speak to her if he saw her with the Browns. Ireland is a very small country, and gossip had a way of coming back to get you.

Just a few steps off the street down to the beach, it was quiet, and you could not hear the traffic up on the street. Right, Danni first. He was not happy about not seeing her this evening, but she talked him down and promised to meet him discreetly the next day.

It had not entered her head that the Browns could have seen them together, until now. How stupid.

Alice didn't answer her phone, so Ruth left her a message inquiring about Tom and how the flight was, also that she had run into the Browns and was having dinner with them, and then said goodbye. Alice would ring back in her own time. Dennis could wait until she was back at her apartment, and then she could have a proper chat with him.

Karen was delighted that she had something to tell her. Her sister knew of Tom Connolly, through the GAA. A lovely man, her sister said. "I was telling her all about the two lovely ladies we met from Kilkenny. What does your husband do, Ruth?"

"I suppose I couldn't just get up and run away from this interrogation", she thought. She decided to just answer the questions until she could leave. That was it! She would say that Dennis would be ringing her and she wanted to be back when he called, so no time for dessert. The only time Len spoke was to say, "I am paying for this, Ruth. No arguments now". She smiled at him and thanked him sincerely.

Everything was the same on the way back, but somehow it had all changed. Karen Brown had coloured things.

Ruth sat in the apartment now, with nothing to do but think. "Yes, I am on holiday, but that doesn't change who I am. Ruth Cullen, a married woman, and best friend of Alice, is suddenly racked with guilt."

She had been reckless with Danni Garcia, walking around like a lovesick puppy as if she were on another planet. Without the thought of being seen by someone from home, how could she explain sitting on the street drinking cocktails with a strange and very handsome man, the first man who had shown interest in her in twenty years and was taken in by him, no matter what his intentions?

As for her friend, Alice had needed her, and she could have been more supportive. Time to put the kettle on. Opening a bottle of wine had become normal since arriving here, but right now, tea was in order. Some fences needed mending, starting with her husband. Sure that he would be home as usual, she dialled their landline, and it was answered almost immediately by a woman. Ruth thought that she had the wrong number, and then the woman asked if the caller wanted to speak to Dennis. "Yes, I do", answered Ruth curtly.

"Okay, hold on." The woman called Dennis.

"Yes?" said Dennis as if he was not expecting a call, and, of course, he wasn't.

"Oh, hi, Ruth. How are you and why the landline?"

"No particular reason. Who is the woman?"

"Just a few from the office here for a few drinks."

It was clear that he had been drinking. "You know how it is when the cat's away." He laughed.

"So how is life in the sun? Are you happy there on your own? Is it very hot? Are you going out later?" So many questions, it hardly gave Ruth time to ask any of her own.

"Who is there?" How many people were going around in her home, making a mess, looking at things, perhaps going from room to room. In the end, she asked how many were at the party?

"Six or seven, all from the office. Don't worry, they won't wreck the place", said Dennis with a big laugh. There was no more to be said.

"Okay, have a good time."

"You too. Bye."

Ruth was shocked and surprised at the notion of her husband having a party while she was away. "Fuck the tea, I will have wine." All these strangers in her house, without her to keep them in order. How dare he. A party? He never normally wanted a party, in all the years they had been married. What was so different now, except that she was away?

Chapter 17

Alice had to play the part of the wife now, no matter how she felt. Holly had gone back to college, and it was good to have the house to herself. Making small talk would have been intolerable, but not long after she got up, her phone rang.

It was Mike. It was so good to hear his voice, and his concern for her came through loud and clear. They chatted for ten minutes before the house phone rang. It was the hospital, she told Mike, and he rang off, saying, "I will call you this evening", and ending with, "I love you, Alice".

"Mrs Connolly, this is the Cardiac Unit at the hospital, just to let you know that your husband is about to go for some scans now and we hope to know more about his condition when you come in this evening. He asked that you not come in the afternoon, because they won't have any information for you and he didn't want to put you to the trouble of making the trip twice."

"Or maybe Ann is going there in the afternoon", thought Alice. Not that she cared how many women visitors he had. Farm Relief Services was looking after the business, giving her time to go and unpack, or so she thought, but the phone kept her busy, her daughters, Sarah, and Ruth, one after the other. She told them all the same thing, except for Ruth.

It was funny to tell her about Ann Nolan, sitting holding Tom's hand, and Mike telling her that he loved her. "Who would have thought it? There is another woman and I don't give a shit", laughed Alice.

"Who is this woman?" asked Ruth. "Do I know her?"

"Probably not. She works in Waterford and only comes home for GAA meetings. But then how do I know that they don't meet every week."

"Anyway, how is Lanzarote without me? Any sign of your gorgeous waiter?"

"No", lied Ruth, "but I did meet Karen, your dancing friend, and she was able to tell me that someone from her area knows Tom. She also got all the info on your return. I swear, Alice, I couldn't think of lies to tell her. The questions were coming at me so fast. So I told her that I was expecting a call and took off."

"Oh my God, I forgot about her. I wonder if she saw Mike and me together."

"Who knows, Alice? Anyway, you have enough on your plate now, so don't give it another thought."

"What is the story with Tom? Is it serious, do you think?"

"I don't know, I will find out this evening when I visit."

"Imagine, Ruth, my husband is sick and I don't give a damn, and it all happened so fast, or maybe not. It was meeting Mike and seeing what life could be like. That is what made me see that Tom and I had no relationship worth talking about. Okay, I had better go and get myself ready to go. You go and enjoy the sun while you can. Talk later."

As she was about to leave the house, Mike texted her. "Hope you are okay; I will ring you later, XX."

Alice just answered, "Okay. X". As she drove to the hospital, her mind was all over the place. What was she going to be told? Was Tom sick, and would she have to spend the rest of her life looking after him? He was not in his bed when she got there. Perhaps he had gone to the bathroom. She sat on the only chair by the bed and waited. Five minutes passed before she decided to go and ask a nurse.

"I am sorry, Mrs Connolly, your husband is not back from his scan yet."

"Thank you, Nurse. I will go and sit in the car for a while."

The nurse took her phone number and promised to ring her when he was back. Time to ring her daughters now and let them know where their dad was at. The girls thought the sun shone out of Tom and would be horrified if they knew what she had done in Lanzarote. They were sharing an apartment in Dublin, so one call was enough; they were all on speaker. Holly seemed very concerned about her dad since she was with him when he was unable to move about and she called the ambulance. Eva was the younger one and thought it was just a glitch. "All old people get them", she said.

"Dad is not old', replied Holly.

"Calm down now, girls. I'm sure your father will be right as rain in no time. I had better end this call now, in case the nurse is trying to ring me."

It was almost an hour before Alice got the call. The time gave her time to focus on why she was there. Tom was attached to a monitor, and the doctor looked concerned. Mrs Connolly, your husband has acute heart failure. Alice sat down, looked at the man in the bed, and felt real pity for him. He looked shocked.

The doctor was speaking to them, but they were not listening. It was Alice who broke the silence. "I'm sorry, can you please repeat what you just said?" She reached for Tom's hand. "What does it mean for my husband in the future? Will he be on medication? Will he be able to work the farm?"

Dr Sexton sat on the end of the bed and explained the condition in detail and told them the shocking facts about Tom's condition. He would be kept in the hospital until he was more stable, then home to be looked after. It was not going to be easy for either of them, and, yes, it was terminal.

Alice couldn't wait to get to the relative safety of her car, where she could cry. She would have to tell the girls, they would be devastated, and she would ask them to come home. Then she thought of Mike. Oh, Mike, there was no hope for them now, no chance for her to get away, and she thought her heart would break. She would have to tell him tonight that it was over.

Chapter 18

Ruth texted Alice to find out how Tom was, but she got no answer. She was probably driving and would be in touch when she was ready. No doubt Tom was okay anyway, and there was a party going on at her house, so she may as well meet Danni. If they met upstairs in the bar, it would seem like an accident.

Danni arrived on time, and they sat at the bar. The same barman had served them before and knew the wine that Ruth liked. Danni had a large beer (what we would call a pint), and they were no sooner seated than he reached for her hand. He then proceeded to place their entwined hands on the bar, not exactly what she wanted.

Everything was different now since she had become aware of other people around them, and all the joy and silliness of last week was gone. Nevertheless, his big tanned hand felt good, warm, and comforting, like he could protect her from everything and everyone. He spun around on his seat and looked seriously into her face. "Ruth, will you stay?"

"Stay, you mean not go home, to my job, my friends, family, and my husband. Danni, you know I can't do that. People don't go on holiday and not come back unless they are teenagers. I didn't come here looking for romance. It was just time out from home and rain and work, and then I met you and got carried away."

That was where he cut in, "Yes, and I met you and fell in love. You are all I think about, Ruth, all day, every day, and I want you in my life. Irish and Spanish, we are good together. We laugh, we make love, and we could work together in my restaurant. It would be our business. Do you make love with your husband as we do? I think not. We are good for each other, you and me."

He was making sense, she knew that, but it was impossible, unthinkable, but it did sound good. Just imagine working here beside him, instead of the tourist office in Thomastown. Oh my God, the wine was going to her head. Danni leaned across and kissed her, and all she wanted to do was touch him, put her hand inside his shirt. She wanted him to make love to her. "Come on down to my apartment." She didn't have to ask twice.

Danni slowed her down, insisting on undressing her slowly and sensually, then made her wait for him to do the same. Not a word was uttered as he joined her on the bed and took her very slowly to new heights of passion. They lay in each other's arms on the small bed. "Now, Ruth, tell me that you don't want that every day—" he laughed "—for as long as we are able". There was no answer. Of course she did, but she kept quiet.

He ran his hand down over her hip and onto her leg, then stopped suddenly. "Why did you stop? I was enjoying that."

"You have a lump in there." He took her hand and brought it to a stop on her outer thigh. "Can you feel it?" he asked.

"Yes, now that you have pointed it out, I can."

His face was serious now. "You need to have it checked out."

"I will as soon as I get home."

"You must promise me."

"Yes, I promise."

"I understand that you are going to go back, but we are not over." He kissed her in a gentle but firm way that made her cry.

"I am so sorry that I must go."

Danni got out of bed and began to get dressed. Ruth's expression said, "Why?"

"I am already way too involved with you, my Irish beauty, so I need to prepare myself for when you are gone. I am going back to the restaurant, and I will try not to think about you so much."

Not knowing if she would ever see him again, Ruth cried herself to sleep. The next morning, with puffed eyes—just as well, she could wear her sunglasses—it was time to go and see Mike. He must be like her, lonely and broken-hearted.

With just one glance at him, it was obvious that something was amiss. Without asking, she sat beside him at an outdoor table. A waiter came, and she ordered an orange juice. Mike could see that Ruth didn't know what Alice had to say, so he told her the story, ending with, "And she never told me".

"She didn't want to upset you until you got home, not as if you can do anything about it."

"Alice rang me at two in the morning. I hoped it was because she was missing me, but it was to say goodbye." His eyes filled up, and he turned away and went to get himself a drink. She had not seen him drink whiskey before; he was very upset.

"I was already planning a trip to Kilkenny, hoping to meet her for a few hours. How did this happen to a man my age, sixty-two years old and feeling like a teenager? Why couldn't we have met under different circumstances, or at home maybe?" Ruth wished that she could comfort the poor man, but what could she say? Then it hit her. She wanted to go home. Alice did need a friend now. She and Mike exchanged numbers and promised to stay in touch.

Luckily there was a flight that very evening. Ruth informed reception that she was leaving early and booked a taxi to the airport. She decided not to tell Danni; she didn't want to say goodbye to him or have him trying to persuade her to stay.

A quick text to Alice, "I have seen Mike and he filled me in. I will be home tonight and will ring you then. XX".

Chapter 19

"Hello, Alice. How are you?"

"In shock", answered Alice. "I was so sure that it couldn't be anything serious, but it is heart disease that is going to kill him."

"Have you told the girls yet?"

"Yes, they are here for a few days, trying to come to terms with the news. I needn't tell you that they are devastated."

"Okay", said Ruth. "I will leave you be with them and we can talk tomorrow."

"Thanks, Ruth. Call over tomorrow".

After the phone call to Alice, Dennis asked if Ruth would like tea or wine. "Wine please." He was waiting for his wife to ask all about his impromptu house party, but she had forgotten all about it.

"Tom Connolly is very sick. He has acute heart failure."

"Oh, how bad is that?" asked Dennis.

"It is going to kill him," replied Ruth, and then there was silence.

Eventually, Dennis said, "But what about a bypass or something?"

"No. There is nothing they can do for him. Alice will have to give up her job and look after him."

***

Ruth was making coffee for both of them, while Holly and Eva were gone to the hospital. They needed to see for themselves how their dad had changed so quickly.

Alice was sitting at the kitchen table with her head down. "What am I going to do? I can't run the farm on my own. When I think of all the time I have spent wishing him gone . . ." Tears rolled quietly down her cheeks. "We never discussed what we would do when we got old and couldn't work anymore. We were too young, or so we thought. Now, look at us."

Alice had leaflets from the hospital outlining what she could be facing while looking after him. As they read through them, Sarah breezed in. "Hello, Ruth. I didn't know that you were back from your holidays."

"Well, when I heard the news, I knew that I had to be here with her." Sarah stood there with her mouth open, waiting to be told the "news". Her sister told her to sit down and explain everything. "Oh my God, and I thought that Ann Nolan was the problem."

"Oh, to hell with her", Alice quipped. "We have real problems. Can you two help me get the front room ready to be made into a bedroom for Tom?"

The three women got to work clearing out the front room and putting the furniture in different rooms. It never occurred to them that the day might come when they would not be able to get upstairs again. And there was still one question that no one was ready to ask.

When they were taking a rest, Sarah asked her sister if she would need to sleep in the same room. "I never thought of that", said Alice.

Sarah continued with the questions, "Will you need help? Will he be able to move around?"

Alice didn't have the answers to most of the questions. "I will know more tomorrow when the palliative care nurse comes here to talk to me."

"Palliative care?" echoed Ruth. "Surely he is not that bad."

"Yes", said Alice, "he is that bad. That's what acute heart failure can do. When Holly took him to the hospital, he was not able to stand up properly. I couldn't believe my ears when the doctor told me that it was just palliative care from now on".

"Did they say how long?"

"No, but probably not more than a year, possibly much less."

"Oh, Alice, I am so sorry. You know I will be here for you", Ruth said.

"Me too," said Sarah. They heard the car coming into the yard, which meant that the girls were back. That conversation was over, and it was time for Sarah and Ruth to leave. They hugged each other and left, all holding the tears in.

Before they got into their cars, Sarah looked at Ruth. "How is this going to work? They can't afford to pay for the farm to be run full-time. Surely not, and anyway, it looks like she will have a full-time job looking after Tom. We will talk to her about it tomorrow when she knows more."

On her way home, Ruth's phone rang again. She knew who it was, so she pulled over and answered it. "Why, Ruth, did you just run away? How was this going to be explained?"

"Danni, I never agreed to stay, and I had no choice but to go. Alice's husband is very ill. She needs me here."

"You could have told me."

"Yes, but to be honest, I couldn't bear to say goodbye to you, Danni. But I am home now, and we must get on as if it never happened."

"As if it never happened?" He was shouting now. "Ruth, I love you."

She wanted to say it back, but that would just make it more difficult. She ached to see him right now, to walk hand in hand with him, to kiss him and make love with him. There was silence, and he knew that she was crying. "I'm sorry darling, but there is no hope for us."

Chapter 20

Ruth had almost a week of her annual leave left to help Alice. Tom Connolly was brought home to his native Barrycastle by ambulance. It was a shocking sight to see the big strong man reduced to a wheelchair covered in a blue blanket. Alice cried when she saw him, and Ruth was there to comfort her.

"He will be okay; we will get him back to normal again soon."

"No", said Alice, "I must accept this now. This is my future, caring for him day and night. I never thought for one minute that Tom could be sick. How am I going to manage the farm when my job is gone? Is this my fault for leaving him and going off to enjoy myself, Ruth?"

One of the paramedics broke into her conversation, "Now, Mrs Connolly, he is comfortable, and a nurse will call later to help you learn how to cope with this new situation". The two women looked at each other. They were meant to be on holiday; now it was like a dream that they shared. Ruth felt that she should give them some privacy, so she left.

Yes, the holiday had left both women in a mess, some of it their own making. Why did they think that they could go off and meet other men and not have to pay the price? The best thing Ruth could do now was to help Alice as much as she could. It might ease the guilt she felt over Danni and not trying to stop Alice from going to stay with Mike.

Dennis understood why his wife spent so much time trying to help her friend. The word was out now that Tom Connolly was seriously ill, and other farmers from the Barrycastle area came to help on the farm and do anything they could to make life easier for Alice.

Ruth spent as much time as possible cooking and cleaning, while Alice spent all her time with Tom. Ruth wondered if she was in contact with Mike but didn't dare ask. Her guilt prevented her from even talking about the holiday. She also felt bad about not telling her friend about Danni Garcia, who had phoned her a few times, insisting that they were not over forever.

One day while Alice was washing Tom, he fell out of the bed, as she had forgotten to put up the rail on the other side of the bed. She rang Ruth to come quickly and help her get him up. Ruth grabbed her car keys and dashed to help. There was no time to get her bag or her phone.

Tom was a big man, but they had been taught how to act in a situation like this, and the two women got him back into bed. Poor Tom felt so bad for having to wait for another woman to help him to bed. Alice was at her wit's end and crying like a child. Ruth told her to go and have a cup of tea while she made Tom comfortable and assured him that it was no big deal for her to help him.

When she was finished, he asked her to sit down. After a long pause and appearing lost for words, he said, "Ruth, I don't know what to do about Alice and the girls".

"What do you mean, do about them?" said Ruth, puzzled.

"How will they manage when I am gone, the farm and all the work it takes? Alice won't be able to do it, and the girls won't be interested in it anyway.

"Tom, there is no need for you to worry about that now. We will think of something. You just concentrate on getting well."

"Ruth! I am not getting any better than I am now, and I don't want her to have to sell it off for next to nothing. You know that there are plenty out there who would take advantage."

Ruth knew that he was right. This was the problem with not having a son to take over. "Tom, let me do some research. I know that the help you have now is temporary and expensive. I will help you put something in place and set your mind at rest."

Back in the kitchen, Alice was crying like a baby. "And to think all I had to worry about was Anna Nolan. Now I wish he was just having an affair; I could deal with that."

"Don't worry, sweetheart, we will think of something. Don't talk to anyone about this, and don't mention selling the farm. You do all the accounts, don't you?"

"Yes", answered Alice.

"So you just need someone you can trust to do the work that Tom did." Ruth stood up to go, putting her hand on Alice's shoulder. "You just concentrate on Tom. I will talk to Dennis about finding someone. He will be discreet."

Chapter 21

As Ruth drove home, her phone rang. She pulled over, thinking it might be Alice, but it was Danni. He insisted that he could not just forget her. Ruth told him about Tom and the situation and that she could not think about them now. He said how sorry he was for her having to deal with the situation and for Alice too. He promised that when they were sorted out, he would be coming to Kilkenny. He had to see her again.

When she put the phone down, the thoughts of him came flooding back, and for a moment she wished that she was still in Lanzarote with him. She had to reign in these thoughts; it was a holiday fling, nothing else.

Dennis was at home when she got there. He was cooking dinner for them, steaks, her favourite, but between Alice and Danni, it was difficult to enjoy her meal. After they had finished eating, Ruth remembered the party and began to question Dennis about it, how it came about, who was there, and what time it ended. What made him decide suddenly become so socially inclined?

She had a million questions, and her husband was giving nothing away. He had never given her any reason to be suspicious before, but this was different. Would he have told her if she had not had to ring that night? In the end, he stood up from the table and looked down at her. "What is the problem with me having some people here for drinks? You were away in the sun for two weeks." There was no more said, but this was not going away, and that was for sure.

There was an uneasy silence between Dennis and Ruth as they sat watching television until her phone rang. It was Mike. "I am sorry to bother you, Ruth, but Danni told me about Alice. How are she and Tom? I want to jump on a plane and come to her, but I doubt that she would see me. I could help her Ruth. Farming is in my blood, as you know."

"Thanks, Mike, I will keep you in mind, but what about your bar?"

"I would get someone to run it. Alice is more important to me."

"I might have to tell a lie or two Mike, but you are a man from Galway and you can do farm work. No need for anyone else to be told anything. Are you sure about this, Mike?"

"I was never surer about anything."

"Okay, should I talk to Alice about it first?"

"Yes, it would be unfair to just land on her door. Please assure her that I would not put in or out of her daily routine. I would be happy doing what I love. The only thing I would need is a room close to the farm."

When the call ended, Dennis wanted to know who it was. "It was a farm labourer who might be right to help Alice and Tom. A friend at work put me on to him. Tom will have to pass him first, of course. I hope he is right for the job; it would be a load off Tom's mind. He is very worried about the future for Alice and the girls."

Dennis hopped up out of his chair. "Is Tom dying then?"

She looked at him seriously. "Yes, Dennis, he is. Now keep that to yourself. The last thing they need is everyone wondering what will happen to the land. You know what they are like around here."

He looked at her innocently. "Sure, whom would I tell?"

Ruth bit back, "How would I know whom you might tell? Someone in your new circle maybe?"

"Oh, give over, will you? They were all colleagues."

"How come I never met them? You said that they were a bunch of bores and I wouldn't like them. They didn't sound boring the night they were here. Were they all couples?"

"Yes, well, some were single, others married."

"Did anyone stay the night?"

Clearly angry now, Dennis said, "No, they didn't, and I won't be questioned about it anymore".

The following morning, on her way to Alice and Tom's, Ruth went over it in her mind. Should she tell Alice first or go straight to Tom. She felt sure that her friend would reject the idea out of hand, before even considering what a good idea it was.

Okay, talk to Alice first. Surprised to find Holly in the kitchen, Ruth hugged her and went to put the kettle on. "When did you arrive?" Ruth asked her.

"This morning", answered the young woman. "I had to see Mam and try and help her out. I will stay at home if necessary. College can wait. What do you think, Ruth?"

"Hold on now, Holly. I have an idea, but I must speak to your parents first."

Alice came from Tom's room.

"How is he today?" Ruth asked.

"The same", said Alice in a dejected voice.

"Okay, have a cuppa and we will go for a walk. I have something to put to you. Holly will look after her dad, won't you?"

Holly agreed.

"So what is so secret that we had to get out of the house for it?" Alice asked her once they were away from the house.

After a long pause, Ruth said, "I have found someone to run the farm for you".

Alice stopped walking and turned to her friend. "Oh, how did you do that? Who is he, and where is he from?"

"He is from Galway and grew up farming, but it was left to his brother. Now he runs a pub but would love to get back to the land. Shall I tell you his name?"

"Go on."

"Mike Wall."

Alice stopped walking. "Do you mean my Mike?" Then she corrected herself. "No, he is not mine!"

"Alice, what are you on about?"

Now it was time for Ruth to come clean. "I was talking to Danni Garcia, and I told him about Tom. I had no idea that he would tell Mike."

"Do you mean Danni the waiter?"

"Yes, but he was not just a waiter. He is the owner, and I was seeing him while you were with Mike." Alice needed to sit down. Ruth steered her towards a wall that they could sit on. "Mike got my number from Danni and phoned me last night. Look, Alice, of course, it is up to you, but he would be a blessing for you and the girls. He could do all the stuff that Tom did and leave you free to look after Tom. You could trust him, and no one would be any the wiser. He could be just a man you employed to run the business. You need have very little to do with him."

"Ruth! Have you lost the plot or what? You are asking me to employ a man that I slept with and act as if it is all normal and above board while I look after my dying husband? No. That can't happen. It would be wrong on so many levels."

"So, do you have a better plan? Anyway, it was not my idea; it was Mike's. Look at it simply, he is a farmer, and you need someone just like him. You can't carry on as you are. It is costing a fortune. These people are for filling in for a weekend, not full-time."

"What could I tell Tom and the girls?"

"Easy, that he is a friend of a friend of mine, from Galway. Introduce him to your family and let Tom decide, if it makes you feel better. They will probably get on well, and it will put his mind at rest."

Chapter 22

Despite, what was happening with her friend, somewhere in the back of her mind, Ruth couldn't get that party out of her head. The man she had married all those years ago was not a party animal, or at least showed no sign of it. Just as she pulled into the front of their house, the phone rang.

It was Danni. "Hello, my love."

"Danni, please stop saying that. I cannot be your love. I am married, remember?"

"Have you been to see your doctor about that lump I found?"

"No, I forgot about it," admitted Ruth.

"Your husband didn't find it then?" It came out as sarcasm.

"No, he didn't get the chance." She had not meant to give him that information.

"Please Ruth, have it checked out tomorrow. I am worried about you."

"Yes, I will do it, but you have no right to worry about me. Danni, don't ring me again", and she ended the call.

Before going inside, she phoned and made an appointment for the next day.

The atmosphere in the house was not good, and she didn't mention the appointment to Dennis, nor did she think about it again that night. After an evening of watching television and not a word spoken, Dennis broke the silence when he said, "I am going to bed". Ruth made him no answer.

When she did go up to their bedroom, Dennis appeared to be sleeping, almost hanging out of his side of the bed. This was not normal for them. They seldom fought, and it never lasted long. When she was settled at her side, she ran her hand down the side of her left leg and felt the considerable-sized lump that Danni had found. Then her mind switched to the feeling of him beside her, their bodies entwined, and she cried herself to sleep.

***

While waiting to be called into the exam room, Ruth texted Alice and promised to call to see her on the way home. She didn't tell her friend where she was. It would be just another thing for Alice to worry about. Then it was her turn to be seen by her doctor of many years. Dr Allen knew that Ruth Cullen had to be there for a good reason. Having examined her leg, he went to confer with his colleague, who confirmed what Dr Allen considered to be the next step. "Ruth, I am sending you straight to the hospital in Kilkenny for an MRI scan. We need to get a closer look at that lump."

Back in her car, she just sat there, looking at her phone. Who could she contact? If only she had a sister or her mother was still alive or Alice didn't have so much to deal with right now. The words *lump* and *MRI* put the fear of God into most people, and Ruth was no different. Even if there was someone with her, the result would be the same. It was time to pull herself together now and get to the city.

More tests, the usual, a biopsy, and so on. A week on, and she had told no one, not even Dennis. Things between them had not improved one little bit. If anything, they had worsened. It was as if he knew that she had been unfaithful, but of course, he didn't. She had no idea what was going on in his life, and right now, she didn't care. It was one appointment after another and still not a definite answer. Then came a meeting with an oncologist, not a surprise to Ruth. She had seen it happen before; it was cancer.

She decided to confide in Sarah, even though she was also trying to help Alice with Tom. Sarah said that they were getting some man to do the farm work, "from Galway, I believe. You will have to tell her; you know that, don't you, Ruth?"

"Yes, but not yet. She has enough to cope with."

She and Sarah sat at a desk, and the oncologist introduced herself. "Josephine Flemming is my name, and I will get you through this. Put my number on your phone, call me Jo, and if you need me, I will answer or call you back. Okay, Ruth?"

"Thank you, Jo." Then out came the file with all the results.

Jo went through the file and began to talk. Sarah caught Ruth's hand, but nothing could change the words. "I am sorry, Ruth, it is cancer, a sarcoma. My colleagues and I believe that we can remove it entirely and follow up with chemotherapy. We would like to admit you as soon as possible. A bed will be arranged for you for Monday."

The women looked at each other as if seeing for the first time. Ruth let out a sound like a wounded animal, and Sarah put both arms around her. "It will be okay, you'll see", she told Ruth.

"I will have to tell Alice now", and as an afterthought she said, "and Dennis. I will need you with me when I tell her. Is that okay Sarah?"

"Sure", said Sarah. "We will go there now."

Alice was in the kitchen when they got there. "I will go to see Tom", said Sarah, "and let you two talk".

"Sounds ominous", said Alice as they both sat down at the kitchen table.

"I have cancer", blurted out Ruth.

Alice was stuck for words. "Where? When? How do you know? Are you sure?"

"Yes, I have just been to the hospital to see an oncologist. It is a sarcoma on my thigh. They are removing it on Monday, then chemo."

"Is it the kind that spreads?" asked Alice.

"I don't know. I don't want to know. Oh, Alice, the thought of chemotherapy scares the life out of me."

"Have you told Dennis?"

"No, he has been acting weird since I got back, not speaking to me. Does he know?"

"No! How could he?"

"He had a party while I was gone and doesn't want to talk about it."

"Your Dennis had a party! That's strange, not like him at all."

"I know, and to be honest, Alice, I don't give a shit. I have enough to be going on with. How is Tom? Any word from the farmhand?" and they both laughed.

"Yes, he will be here in a day or two, and Tom can interview him and so on. If Tom approves of him, it will be between them. Purely business."

"Yeah!" laughed Ruth, glad of something else to talk about. "So you have been talking to him, then?"

"Yes, briefly. That's the way it must be, Ruth, and I am depending on you to stick to the rules when I introduce you to him."

"I hope that they get on well. It will give Tom peace of mind and be one less thing to worry about."

Then Alice looked sad. Ruth reached over and caught her hand and said, "What a mess. It is like yesterday when we didn't worry about the world as we set off on holiday, and look at us now".

"What time are you going in on Monday?"

"Nine o'clock."

"How long have you had the lump?"

"I don't know. It was Danni who found it."

Alice clasped her hand over her mouth. "I had forgotten what you told me about him. With Tom, worrying about our future, I forgot about you. Thank God he found it. Let's hope they get it all now. Have you been in touch with him since?"

"Yes, it was him who reminded me to have it seen to. He insists that he loves me."

"And how do you feel about him?"

"To be honest, Alice, I don't know."

"I wish that we had never met. My life would be so much simpler. I never knew how much I liked having sex until I had it with him. Now I can't get it out of my mind. However, I will go now and get my head right for Monday. An interesting week ahead, my friend."

"Yes", said Alice as she came around the table and hugged Ruth.

Chapter 23

On the short drive home, the word *sarcoma* was going around in Ruth's brain. What was it, where did it come from, and could it spread to other parts of her body? She would have to look it up before Dennis got home. He would have a lot of questions, so she would do the research.

Hell-bent on what she had to do, Ruth didn't notice the envelope on her kitchen worktop. She trawled through one website after another and looked at all the possible outcomes of a sarcoma. She was none the wiser when she finally gave up on Google.

She decided to make a good dinner. It would keep her mind occupied and give her time to decide how to tell Dennis the bad news. She had two lovely steaks in the fridge and made a good pepper sauce to go with it, together with fresh chips and onions, his favourite. Now, this felt normal.

Everything was ready for when he arrived. He was a bit late, so Ruth poured herself a glass of wine while waiting, then another one. Not like him to be this late, she would ring him to find out if he would be home soon.

The phone rang out, so she tried again. "He must be driving." This time he answered.

"Yes", that was all he said.

Taken aback, she asked, "Will you be long? I have dinner ready".

"Dinner? Did you not get the letter?"

"Dennis, what are you talking about? What letter?"

"Ruth, I am not coming home. Find the letter and read it."

The line went dead.

Looking around the kitchen, she spotted an envelope by the kettle. How come she had not seen it before? She went to the living room, sat on her side of the sofa, and opened the letter. This was the first time Dennis had written to her.

It said:

Dear Ruth, I am sorry for not telling you face-to-face, but I have met a woman and she means the world to me. She is a widow, and I am going to live with her. I will not be asking for my interest in our house, so you can sell it if you want to. I'm sure you'll agree that the spark is well gone from our marriage and we both need to move on. Nancy and I wish you all the best in the future.

Dennis

Another glass of wine and a warm throw from the back of the sofa. Ruth curled up into the foetal position. Too numb to cry, she just stayed there sipping the wine until sleep took over. It was bright when she woke up, and her head was pounding. The empty wine bottle beside her on the sofa answered that question. Then the memories came flooding back; the letter was also there beside her.

How did she not see this coming? There must have been signs. What sort of fool was she? Almost falling to the floor and not wanting to stay there, Ruth made her way to the bedroom, their bedroom. No, it was now her bedroom. Dennis was gone, no fighting, no rows, just gone. "It is Saturday and I am having a cancer operation on Monday. Should I ring and tell him? He is still my husband, my next of kin. He is the person that they will ring if I don't make it on Monday."

Finally, the tears flowed, but there was no one to hear her crying, so she let it all out. Her husband was gone with another woman, and she had cancer. How much worse could it get?

Her bag was packed for her hospital stay; it was as if someone else had done it. She drove herself, not wanting to tell her friends that Dennis was gone. She had a little giggle to herself when deciding to leave him as her next of kin. It would serve him right if he got the call to say that she had died on the operating table. Not that she cared much herself.

Alice and Sarah assumed that Dennis was at the hospital with her, so they just waited for him to call and say that it went well. The operation did go well, as far as the doctor was concerned, but this was just the beginning of her treatment. She thanked the doctor without really listening to him.

Chapter 24

Alice had no idea what Ruth wanted to tell her, but she feared the worse. Thankfully Holly was home to look after Tom. It was unusual to have anyone but next of kin visiting after an operation, while still in recovery. Alice was shown in by a very friendly nurse who knew why she was asked for by Mrs Cullen.

Ruth had explained to the staff that her husband would not be joining her and the reason why. Still hooked up to oxygen and other tubes, Alice got a shock and couldn't find any words for her friend. She had so many questions, "Where is your husband?" "How are you feeling?" "What did they do to you?" So she just sat down and held her hand. "Are you okay?" asked Alice. Ruth was still drowsy from the anaesthetic.

"He's gone", she whispered.

"What? Who is gone?"

"Dennis left me, for another woman, left a letter."

Alice was trying to make sense of what her friend was talking about. "Okay", whispered Alice. She could tell her when she was fully awake. "How do you feel, love? Are you in pain?"

Ruth just shook her head. "Just a bit sore and tired."

"Okay, hun, you just sleep for a while. I will be here. I'm going nowhere."

With that, Ruth closed her eyes. The nurse who was close by tapped Alice on the shoulder and advised her to go and get a coffee. Ruth would be asleep for a while.

Where the hell was Dennis Cullen? Did he find out about Danni? How could he? And what was that about another woman? It must have been the medication she was all mixed up with. No doubt Ruth would tell her when she came to. Ruth slept for two hours, and her friend was sitting beside her when she woke up, much brighter now. A nurse came and took her blood pressure and checked on everything. "Now, ladies, you can have a chat, but not too long", she said, looking at Alice. "We don't want to tire her out."

"Are you feeling better now? You were all over the place after the operation. Where is Dennis, and what is this about a letter?"

"He just packed up and left, leaving me a letter saying that he had met someone else and was going to live with her."

Alice couldn't believe her ears; he was the last man she had ever expected to do such a thing. "Did you have any clue that it might be going on?"

"Not a clue", answered Ruth without any emotion.

"Does he know that you are here?"

"No, he left, so why would I think he cared? He must have been thinking about it for a while. He didn't even have the balls to tell me to my face."

"Have the doctors told you how the operation went?"

"No. not yet."

"Do you want me to be here when they do?"

Ruth extended her hand to Alice. "If you wouldn't mind, hun."

"Does Danni know that you are in here?"

"No. I was afraid that he would arrive here."

"I don't suppose you have told him that Dennis is gone? You are going to need someone to help you when you go home. Have you thought about that?"

"No, I haven't. I'm sure I'll be okay. I will probably have crutches for a while. I won't be able to drive, now sounds like more of a problem."

"Not to worry, Sarah and me will be on hand anytime you need us."

"Thanks, Alice. I don't know what I would do without you."

As Alice drove home, she was thankful that her friend did not think to ask about Tom and their new farmhand.

Working with Mike was not going to be easy, pretending not to know him, when all she wanted to do was put her arms around him. She had to stop herself from calling him "love"—not that she saw too much of him. He got on with the farm work and talked to Tom on the phone a lot. Tom was a lot more content since Mike arrived; they got on well from the moment they met.

He found lodgings not far from the farm and had his meals there too. He was known as "the farm manager from Galway". The people from Barrycastle didn't take long to get to know him, and he was quizzed by all who met him. They all told Alice how lucky she was to have found him, and she was, in more ways than one.

They agreed to stay away from each other as much as possible, for Tom's sake and their own, as it would be impossible not to be intimate with each other if they were close to each other during the working day. Looking after her husband was almost a full-time job, but knowing that Mike was close by made it easier for Alice to get through the day.

It would not look strange to anyone if they were seen together. After all, he was working for her, but they both knew that they could not keep their hands off each other if they were alone. They agreed that before he arrived, and even though it was never said, they knew that their time would come and they would be together.

The two daughters liked Mike and would go and chat to him when they were home, and sometimes brought him a cup of coffee. They even asked their mother why Mike didn't come to the house for his meals. Alice answered that she had enough to do without making dinner for the farm manager.

Even Sarah, who was standing at the window looking out at Mike working, commented that he was a fine-looking man. Alice chose to ignore her but thought to herself, "Hands off. He is mine", as she smiled to herself.

Chapter 25

Ruth was told that the operation went well and they believed that they removed the sarcoma entirely, but they would like to follow up with chemotherapy just to be on the safe side.

She looked at Alice and back to the doctor. "Really, is that necessary?"

"Yes, we believe it is. Just to be sure."

"Okay", said Ruth.

The doctor left and the two women looked at each other. "What do you think?" asked Ruth. "Chemo is the last thing I need right now. Surely if it's gone, it's gone. I need to get back to normal life, or what used to be a normal life. I didn't think past the operation."

Alice reached out and caught her hand. "Look, love, I think you should consider it. It may not be too bad, and we will be with you all the way."

"I suppose you are right. Can you take me home tomorrow?"

"Of course I will."

Ruth lay back on her pillows and began to cry. "I can't believe that life could change so much in just a few weeks. Dennis should be here to look after me, in sickness and in health. Isn't that what it was all about? Not that I want him back now. I just never imagined that he would walk away, just like that, no warning whatsoever. I never considered staying with Danni, not for a second." Then with a laugh, she said, "I thought it would kill Dennis if I didn't come back. How wrong was I?"

Alice stood up and hugged her friend. "Come on now, my friend. I need you to get ready to go home. Do a shopping list, and I will get Sarah to do it in the morning. I must go now, but I will phone you later."

After Alice left, and despite her reassurances that all would be well, right now Ruth couldn't see it. She was a deserted wife, with cancer and no one to look after her as she struggled through chemo. She began to cry like never before. How could she have been so stupid not to notice that her husband was having an affair? She must have missed something. No wonder he was happy for her to go on a two-week holiday without him. Then she remembered the phone calls while she was there. What an actor, not a hint of what he was up to. She stopped crying and became angry. "Well, fuck him and his fancy woman." She would get through this without him.

It was Sarah who arrived the next day to take her home. "I have your shopping. Now we will go home and make you a nice meal."

"By the way", said Sarah, "I am staying with you for as long as you need me, unless you throw me out, that is".

Silent tears rolled down Ruth's cheeks. "Thank you, Sarah. You are so good to me, and I don't deserve it."

"Of course you do, Ruth. You did nothing wrong."

Without thinking, she blurted out the story of Danny Garcia, without the feelings she has for him and the contact they have had since she got back. Sarah looked slightly shocked and then laughed. "Imagine you and the Spanish waiter. I bet you are glad now that you had a bit of fun behind his back."

"I could have had more if I knew what Dennis was up to."

"It was Danni who found the lump on my leg."

"Oh my God", said Sarah, "he saved your life".

"Yes, I suppose you could say that." Ruth decided that she had said enough and changed the subject. "It will be great to have you stay for a while. I must go back to the hospital on Friday to arrange for the chemo. I hope they don't want to do too many."

"How are things at work? Are you very busy?"

"Yes", laughed Sarah. "Our best person went on holiday, and we are waiting for her to come back."

Ruth threw her head back and laughed loudly. "She must be having a great time, lucky bitch. Seriously, though, it will be some time before I am back behind that counter."

"Do you want to ring in, or will I do it for you? Of course, you will have to get a doctor's cert."

"Oh, I forgot that. I will do it tomorrow."

Dr Flemming was upbeat as she welcomed Ruth into her office. "It is good news, Ruth, well good as in we appear to have fully removed your sarcoma, but we still want to do the follow-up treatment, just to be sure that it does not return. The treatment will not be too severe, and you should get through it easily enough. The treatment will be radiation therapy and will commence in at least five weeks, by which time your leg should be healed. It will be a low dose, only on the site of the sarcoma."

Ruth found her voice. "No chemo then?"

Dr Flemming smiled. "No, Ruth, you are a lucky lady. I wish I had such good news for all my patients."

Suddenly, everything looked better. "I must tell Danni the good news." Little did she know that Mike was keeping him up to date on everything that was happening and he was waiting with bated breath for a call to say that she was well. He was afraid to keep calling her, just in case she might tell him to stop and never to call again.

Chapter 26

Alice had to be the first to be told the good news. It was Danni that Ruth wanted to tell, but it wouldn't be fair to give him hope when there was none.

Alice and Sarah were delighted to hear the news. Now she had five weeks to relax and maybe go back to work before the treatment. Ruth felt like she had gotten a new lease on life, even though her leg was very sore right now.

It was time to call in to see Tom and see how he was, maybe even meet the farm manager. She giggled to herself. It would be strange seeing Mike working the land instead of his bar in sunny Lanzarote.

Tom was sleeping when she got there, so she had a cup of coffee with Alice. They couldn't talk about Mike because the door to Tom's room had to be open, in case he needed anything. "Do you mind if I go and say hello to Mike if he is close by?" Ruth asked. Alice agreed.

Mike's eyes lit up when he saw her. "You are looking good, Ruth. I heard that you were in the hospital." She wondered who told him but said nothing. "How are you now? Okay, I hope."

"Yes, Mike, I am good, but I must go back for some radiation therapy in the coming weeks. Nothing to worry about. Not like poor Tom. How are you and he getting on, Mike?"

"Very well, thank God. A nice man." Alice's name was not spoken, nor was Danni's. It felt unreal, like they were all taking part in a play.

They should be talking about Lanzarote, the heat, and where they were going tonight because that was what he reminded her of. She wanted to ask about Danni but didn't dare mention his name. For her it was a holiday fling, that was all.

"It must be strange for you to live in Ballycastle, with everyone wanting to know your business", Ruth said.

"Yes", answered Mike, "but I am well able to get around that. I am just glad to be able to help Alice. Plus, I love farming".

After they chatted a bit longer, Ruth made her way back inside the farmhouse.

"Well?" said Alice. "How did you get on with the chat? Did you ask him about Danni?"

"No. I must put that experience behind me now and get on with my changed life as a single woman, living alone."

"I take it you have no word from Dennis?"

"Not a word", answered Ruth. "Imagine he walked out on you and didn't look back." Her eyes were filling up at the thought that she was so easily forgotten.

Alice pushed a fresh cup of coffee towards her. "Now, now. Cry if you want to, but not for him. He is not worth it. Now come into the fire and put your feet up. You must relax to start that leg healing."

Chapter 27

Sarah was not back from work when Ruth returned home. It was nice to have another person in the house, and she was thankful for her friend being there. Getting in and out of the car was a struggle at the moment, and she could just about make the drive to Alice's house. The heating was turned on, and Sarah had made dinner the day before. All she had to do was sit down and read her book and be thankful for her friends.

She couldn't be sure if she missed Dennis or not. Too much had been happening since he left, and the medication made her sleep almost as soon as she got into bed. Some of his stuff was still in the house, and she would pack it up when she felt better and put it in the garage.

Their bed felt different, and she was used to sleeping beside him for so long, she missed the familiarity of her old life, but the thrill of lying beside Danni Garcia was still very fresh in her mind. Trying to imagine if it would turn out the same if she and Danni were together for twenty years, she didn't think so. Not much point in thinking about it, but if she knew that Dennis was cheating on her at the time, things could have been different.

Who the hell was Nancy anyway? Who wished her all the best for the future, and how long had they been together? For the first time she was curious about the woman who had replaced her, and try as she might, she could not concentrate on the book in her lap. The sound of a car driving into the yard was welcome, she was glad that Sarah was home, and now that was the end of the questions about her cheating husband.

Then there was a knock on the door, but Sarah had a key. Ruth got up, put her crutch under her arm, and went to open the door.

Was her mind playing tricks on her, or was Dennis standing there? Ruth looked around to see if Nancy was with him. She was glad of the crutch to hold her up. When she found her voice, words came out automatically. "What are you doing here?"

Now it was him who was dumbfounded. "What happened to you?"

"What do you care?" snapped Ruth.

He looked sort of pathetic. "Can I come in, please?"

"Yes, if it is to collect your belongings and be gone again in ten minutes."

He stepped inside tentatively and walked behind her to the living room. Ruth sat back into the chair and picked up her book as if to carry on reading.

Dennis sat down. "Ruth, I am sorry for what I have done to you."

She stared at him with a cold look that said, "You go on now and explain what it is that you have done". Making no effort at conversation, Ruth knew that she was making this very difficult for him. And to her surprise, she had no wish to make it any easier for him. There was no love or even pity to see him struggling for words to explain why he had abandoned her and their marriage. What did he want? For her to take him back, to pretend the last few weeks never happened?

"Please, darling, we can do this, put it behind us, pretend it never happened."

Just then Sarah came in. He seemed shocked that she had a key. He stood up as if he was going to ask her to leave. Instead, it was Sarah who asked him to leave. "Look, Dennis, Ruth has enough to cope with now without you coming in here hassling." He looked at his wife for confirmation that she had the right to make him leave, and she just looked at him as if to say, "You have been told".

As he was leaving, he looked at Ruth and asked, "What is wrong with your leg?"

It was Sarah who answered him. "She has cancer, now leave her be."

"Cancer!" he almost shouted. "Why didn't you tell me?"

"Why?" said Ruth, in a low voice. "Would you and Nancy have come here to help me?"

After he closed the front door, Sarah said, "Sorry if you didn't want him to know". They both laughed. "I couldn't resist putting the boot in."

"I know, his face was priceless."

As the two women relaxed after dinner, Sarah asked, "What did Dennis want?"

"I don't know. I was so shocked to see him there, and there was so much going on in my head, I didn't listen to him. I was so glad that you came in when you did."

"Surely he is not thinking of coming back, is he?"

"Well, when you consider how he left, nothing would surprise me about my husband."

"No doubt he will be back when I am not here", said Sarah, "so you need to think about whether you want him back or not".

Chapter 28

Alice overheard Tom talking to Mike about ordering food for the animals, and then he said to come in so they could talk about it. "Okay", answered Mike, "as soon as I get finished here".

Knowing that he would knock at the back door, Alice was excited at the thought of just answering her door. As usual, Mike barely looked at her as he went through to the room where Tom was. She was still standing in the hallway for seconds later as Mike came back out. "He is asleep. Are you sure asked, Alice?"

"Come with me", she ordered as they went to Tom's room.

Alice went up close to her husband to check his breathing. Looking back at Mike with relief, "He is okay", she whispered. Without thinking, she asked Mike if he wanted a cup of coffee.

"Yes, please."

They sat one at either side of the table. Mike was the first to speak. "This must be difficult for you."

"Yes, it is, but just knowing that you are out there is a great help. I don't know what I would do if you were still in Spain."

"Sorry, I meant not knowing what you are going to find when you go into his bedroom." Alice was so embarrassed, she could feel the colour rising in her cheeks. Mike saw it too and smiled while stretching his arm across the table and holding her hand. She didn't know whether to laugh or cry.

"Yes, I know what you mean. Both situations are difficult for me. How do you think I feel being so close to you, wanting you so much, and not even chatting to you? Look at how long it has taken for us to have a coffee together."

"Would it be a scandal around here if they knew that we drank coffee together at the kitchen table while your husband was sleeping?"

"Probably", laughed Alice.

Tom heard her and called out. "Any sign of Mike? I asked him to come in".

Alice went in, fixed the bed clothes, and sent Mike in. The two men chatted for a while; Tom was always happy having chatted with Mike. "That man is a God-send", he said when she brought him some of her homemade soup that he loved. It was difficult to find food that he wanted and that he could digest. He didn't have many visitors nowadays and didn't want them. He got all the sporting news from the local paper, which one of his girls got for him on their way home at the weekend.

Then they would sit for a few hours reading and discussing the topics of the week with their dad. Tom loved his daughters and never mentioned that they didn't have a son who would take the farm on when he was gone. It was very important to most farmers.

He surprised Alice one day when he said, "We need to talk about the funeral".

Her reaction was typical, "Oh, stop that kind of talk now, Tom", but he raised his hand to stop her from saying any more.

"We both know that it is coming, and I want everything sorted out for you and the girls. Now, love, get a pen and paper." He gave her a list of dos and don'ts and finished with, "And don't bury my good suit. Give it to a charity", and gave a little laugh.

Alice lay her head on the bed beside him and cried. Tom put his hand on her head. "It's okay, Al. You will manage well, with Mike to help you. I have asked him, and he said yes." Alice lifted her head and looked at him. He was smiling; it was just about the farm.

Before she left the room, she kissed him on the forehead and said, "Thanks, Tom".

This was the husband that she had lived with for twenty-odd years and had two beautiful daughters with. True, her feelings for Mike were different, but Tom had not been a bad husband or father and they had been through good times and bad. Life was now coming to an end, and their children were going to be devastated, even though they knew it was coming.

Chapter 29

Ruth didn't sleep much that night, knowing that Dennis would probably make contact again the next day. What would she say if he wanted to come back? She had been happy enough with him until she met Danni Garcia. The only thing missing from their marriage was sex. Was it that important? She didn't think so at the time.

Was she prepared to go it alone for the rest of her life or meet someone new? God knew what he might be like, the idea of getting to know and maybe living with a different man. Going from one relationship to another, she would be known in Barrycastle as the woman who got dumped. They would watch closely if she spoke to any man, wondering if she was making a play for him.

She hadn't had time to think about all of this since he left and then her cancer diagnosis, but now she was forced to consider what her future might look like. Was she strong enough to go it alone? If a friend asked her for advice in a situation like this, she wouldn't hesitate to say, "Get rid of him". Perhaps she should ask a friend before deciding.

After an almost sleepless night, she was awakened by her phone. It was Dennis texting her. He wanted to see her during the day, but she needed more time to think before meeting him. Tomorrow would suit me better; mid-morning would be okay.

Ruth drove to see Alice and have that chat; she had forgotten to let her know that she was coming to see her. Upon arrival, she knocked on the door. Alice came to open the door for her, and as she did, Ruth heard the back door close. "I am sorry for not texting you. Are you free to chat?"

"Of course, I am always free to talk to you. How is your leg?"

"Good", answered Ruth, "should be ready to go back to work soon. In the meantime, I have another situation to deal with. Dennis arrived yesterday, and I think he wants to come back".

"What will you do?" asked Alice.

"I don't know."

"Do you want him back?"

"Not really, but I don't want to be single for the rest of my life."

"Has he said that he wants to get back to you? Perhaps you should wait and see what he has to say. Maybe he wants a divorce", laughed Alice, squeezing her friend's hand.

"Maybe," said Ruth.

"How would you feel about that?"

Ruth put her head down into her hands and sighed. "Alice, I have spent all night thinking about that, but I must admit I never considered that it might not be my decision to make. Come to think of it, that would be easier. It would save me from making a big decision that I would probably regret." They were interrupted when Tom called out to his wife.

Alice almost ran to the room. She could see him deteriorating by the day. His voice was very low, and he needed more help just turning in the bed.

"Is that Ruth I hear?" he asked.

"It is. Do you want to see her?"

"Ya", he answered, "if she doesn't mind".

Ruth was delighted to see him. She went over to the bed and kissed him on the cheek. Alice standing at the end of the bed said, "Hold on there now you. Don't go upsetting the sick man". They all laughed.

"How are you feeling, Tom?" asked Ruth.

"Not great", he said. Alice left them to go and make tea. "To be honest, Ruth, I hope it does not go on for too long. This is no kind of life for a farmer. Mind you Mike is great and I am very grateful to you for finding him. It is a load off my mind. I know now that they will be all right, and if they decide to sell up, what of it? I told Mike what to do, and I trust him to do right by Alice and the girls."

Chapter 30

Unknown to the women, Mike and Danni were in constant contact, and Danni was keeping an eye on Mike's bar in Lanzarote. He never failed to ask about Ruth and how she was after the operation, and of course, he asked about her husband. Mike didn't know much about that situation; he couldn't ask Alice without causing suspicion, and both women had enough to deal with.

Mike was happy to be close to Alice daily, and that was all due to Ruth. He had the best of both worlds. Apart from Alice, farming was closest to his heart and he had thought about what would happen when Tom passed on. Could he buy the farm and sell the pub, or perhaps Alice would want to keep it. He could see that she was a very capable woman and well able to run the place, with a little help for the heavy work.

Tom had paid him in advance for one month after his death, to keep things running smoothly for his family. The two men got on well, and sometimes Mike felt guilty for loving Alice, but he did, and that was that, and he hoped for a future with her in it. Here or Lanzarote, it didn't matter. He would have to be patient, and it would be her decision.

Danni Garcia showed no sign of forgetting about Ruth. Should he tell him that she had not mentioned his name when they met? Sarah was the one who came out to chat with him sometimes, but he had not seen her around for a while. She was a very nice lady, and he was careful not to be too familiar with her.

As it happened, Mike was driving into the yard in the car that Tom used to do everyday stuff. As Ruth was leaving, they each rolled down the windows and said hello and asked how the other one was. Mike asked Ruth how her leg was and how she was feeling. "I feel good in that respect, Mike. I wish everything in my life was so simple."

"Oh", said Mike, giving her the opening to tell him if she wanted to, and she did. It never dawned on her that he would be in touch with Danni or that Danni would be interested in her life, as she tried not to think about him or the fact that she had had an affair, making her even with Dennis. Mike wished her the best with her predicament and offered to be a listening ear when and if she needed him. She thanked him again for what he was doing for Alice and Tom. Mike smiled and said, "There is no place I would rather be".

Chapter 31

He would be here any minute. It was like waiting for an inspection, and it was a stranger that she was waiting for, not the man she had been married to for so long, shared everything with, some good times and some not so good. But that was life and what she had on holiday was just a fling, pure romance, fantastic sex, not to be compared with real life. No one had sex like that, and if they did, she had never heard of it.

The clothes she wore were carefully chosen: Dennis would not have seen them before. If she was going to be dumped, she would not look like a victim. What if he was going to bring the new girlfriend with him? The very idea made her shake. No, he wouldn't, or would he? After all, she never thought for one minute that he would leave her.

The knock on the door came, and Ruth dallied for a short while before answering. "Come in." She didn't use his name on purpose.

"Hello, Ruth, you are looking good. How are you feeling?"

"I suppose I feel like most women who get dumped after years of marriage. How are you and Nancy getting on?"

"Never mind that, what happened to your leg? Is it cancer?"

"Yes, hardly something we would make up." Taking charge of the situation and looking him straight in the face, "Well! Why are you here?" asked Ruth.

As she waited for Dennis to speak, he looked at the floor and said nothing for a few seconds. Then looking at his wife, as if for the first time, he said, "Can we start again?"

"Start again", replied Ruth. "I never stopped, you did. You had an affair, then left me, so what has changed?"

"I was stupid and I am sorry, so sorry. It must have been difficult for you, and I am sorry for not telling you to your face. You did nothing to deserve that, and I will make up for it if you give me the chance. I do love you, Ruth, always have."

"Yeah, and what about Nancy? Do you love her also?"

"I thought I did, but now I know that it was you all the time."

"Dennis, I don't know if I want you back. Despite what you think, I managed well without you; I have good friends and still have my job."

"But what about cancer? How will you get through that on your own?"

"As I said, I am not on my own."

Ruth stood up. The meeting was over, and he was not getting an answer today. She walked towards the front door, and he followed.

"When can I see you again?"

"I don't know, I need time to make up my mind."

"But, Ruth, surely, it's simple. Do you still love me?" He was on the outside of the house now.

"I will think about it and let you know."

He looked pleadingly at her. "Please say yes. I can't imagine life without you." She had never seen her husband like this before, and she felt sorry for him.

After he had left, Ruth strolled into her kitchen and sat at the table. There was a box of photographs in one of the cupboards. Reaching out from where she was seated, she took the box out and began to look through it. It was their life in photos, from before they got married and when they were in love and trying for a baby.

They went through some tough times when they lost two babies through miscarriage, but it seemed to make them stronger when it would have torn other couples apart. They comforted each other as they accepted that they would not have children. It would be just the two of them forever.

"It was not a bad life", she thought to herself. "We went to events, had weekends away and annual holidays without having to organise babysitters like Alice and Tom, and she enjoyed their girls growing up and coming to visit and sometimes staying over." On seeing a photo of the four friends on a holiday in France together, Ruth remembered that Dennis had not asked how Tom was. This stuck in her mind and set her thinking about him. Did he care about anyone? About the way that he left her, and now is ready to leave Nancy, she wondered if Nancy even knew that he was trying to go back to his old life.

She heard Sarah's car come into the drive but didn't move or stop what she was doing. Sarah sat down beside her and picked up the picture of her sister and husband. Poor Tom, he looked so strong there compared to now. Nudging Ruth, Sarah said, "You are in a funny old mood this evening. How did it go with Dennis? Does he want to come back?"

"Yes, he does, and I am trying to make up my mind if I want him or not."

Chapter 32

Their lives changed that night. It was almost midnight when Sarah came into Ruth's room. In a gentle voice, she said, "Alice just rang. Tom has taken a turn, and the girls are on their way home. I must go to her. Do you want to come?"

"Or perhaps you should get some sleep. If we are up all night, you will be needed tomorrow. Is that okay with you?"

"Yes, sure, you go on and I will see you later. Good night, Sarah." The two women hugged, and Sarah rushed out the door. They all knew that this day was coming, and now it was time to be practical.

It was time now for Alice, Eva, and Holly to be with Tom to say goodbye. Tomorrow would be a busy day at the Connolly household. If Tom had passed, there would be a steady stream of family and close friends calling, and as is the custom here in Ireland, everyone would be offered a cup of tea and a sandwich. Ruth drifted off to sleep while planning tomorrow in her head.

The sound of her phone ringing in the distance was what got her out of a deep sleep. Getting out of bed and stumbling into the kitchen, she was sure that it was about Tom, but was surprised to see Dennis was calling. "Why is he ringing at this time of the morning?" "Good morning", said Dennis when she answered. Ruth was cross that he was on the phone so early, so her answer was, "Yes, what can I do for you?"

"Have you decided yet, love?"

"Dennis, Tom is dying or may be dead by now. I have not given it a single thought, nor will I do so in the coming days. I am going to see the family now, and helping there will keep me busy." While getting dressed, Ruth could not get one word out of her head. He had called her Love. Did her husband even know what love was? she wondered.

Upon reaching Connolly's house, it was difficult to find a place to park. The house, while sombre, was also busy. It was clear that Tom had died during the night. Eva was the first one to cling to Ruth for comfort, wrapping her arms around the girl and whispering, "He's gone then?"

The sobbing girl nodded her head and let the tears flow. "Oh, Ruth, what are we going to do without him? I can't believe that he is gone."

Sitting Eva down, still holding her hand, Ruth tried to reassure her that they would cope and Dad would be there looking out for her. "Now I suggest that you go and find your favourite photo of your dad and keep talking to him. I do believe that he will hear you. I will go to see your mam now. Is she in the room?"

"Yes, and thanks for being here; she is going to need you."

Alice was sitting by the bed, holding Tom's almost cold hand, and Holly was on the other side doing the same. Just sitting, not talking or crying, until Ruth entered, at which point both got up and came to Ruth and all three cried. Tom looked like he was sleeping. "What time did he pass?"

"It was almost six this morning, and it was very peaceful, thank God", said Alice.

Alice went into practical mode then. "Now, Holly, the undertaker will be here shortly to take dad away for a while. Will you and Eva pick out the clothes you would like to put on him, but not his good jacket", laughed Alice. "He wants that to go to the charity shop." They all had a giggle about him not wanting to waste his best jacket.

When Holly left the room, Alice turned to Ruth. "Will you go and see Mike, fill him in, and see if he wants to come in for a cuppa? I have done all I can now for Tom. Does that sound very heartless?"

"To someone else, yes, it would, but I know better." They hugged, like two people who knew each other very well. "OK, you do that. I have some phone calls to make."

Mike was cleaning out the cowshed and about to make himself a cup of coffee. Glad to see Ruth, he stopped what he was doing. "Well, how are things inside? Is she coping?"

"Yes, she is. It was Alice who told me to come and see you and to ask you for tea."

"Are there many people in there?" asked Mike.

"No, just two neighbours now, so you may as well come and meet them. You are the man around here now."

Mike laughed while he couldn't be seen. "Ruth, you are bold." As they were leaving the shed, Mike caught her hand. "Ruth, I should tell you that Danni asks about you every time we talk."

"Do you talk to him often, then?"

"Yes, he is keeping an eye on my place." They were approaching the back door now and had to end that conversation.

Chapter 33

After some gentle persuading, Alice and her daughters agreed to go to bed and get some sleep. Tom's body would not be back for some hours, and they had been up all night. Sarah had gone home, so it was just Ruth to greet callers. Then she thought of Mike; he could help her. He was happy to do what was needed of him.

He handed out sandwiches, answered the door, and talked to the local farmers and their wives. Some tried to find out more about the stranger, but his time in the bar trade stood to him when it came to not giving away too much.

Of course, they wondered if Alice would sell the farm. This was typical of the farming community; they were probably looking into buying it since Tom became ill. If the Connolly's had a son, it would be different. Or if one of the girls were married, but he would have to be from farming stock

Throughout the day Mike heard snippets of conversation, all wondering the same thing while standing in the woman's kitchen eating what they could. Other people dropped off cakes and more sandwiches and bottles of wine and whiskey and refused to come in, saying, "Sure ye have a full house. Tell Alice that I called".

It was late in the afternoon when Mike answered the door. He had no idea who the man standing there was. "Come in, I'm afraid Alice is having a lie down now, but Ruth is here." Turning around quickly when she heard her name being mentioned, her mouth fell open when she saw Dennis. Mike had no idea who Dennis was, so Ruth had no choice but to introduce them and address him as her husband.

The tension was palpable between them, and Mike picked up on it quickly. He offered to get Dennis a drink. "Yes, tea, please."

"Are you okay, love?" asked Dennis. There it was again; it made her angry. How dare he use that word, making it sound as if they were a happy couple. Everyone around here knew that he left her for another woman, but today was no time to make a scene. Thankfully Sarah came back, and Ruth took a few minutes out and went out to her car. It would be time to get the girls up soon.

Remembering what Mike had said earlier about Danni Garcia, still thinking about him set her mind spinning. If only it were him in there instead of Dennis, she wouldn't want to leave his side. The images came flooding back, of him sitting at the hotel bar waiting for her and how she felt at the very sight of him, the passion that he aroused in her, sexual feelings that she thought were long gone and she was no longer capable of. Dennis interrupted her thoughts. "There you are", he said as he came around the corner from the back door. "Who is this Mike fella? He seems very much at home here."

Ignoring the question, Ruth said, "Never mind, Mike. Why are you here?"

"I am here to support you, love."

She raised her voice, "Will you stop calling me love? Stop pretending that we are back together, Dennis. You have no business here, and I want you gone before Alice and the girls come down. All the time while Tom was ill, where were you? You never once asked how he was. Now fuck off".

***

Alice was up and dressed when Ruth went to call her. "The undertaker just called; they will be here in an hour. Where do you want the coffin?"

"In the sitting room, I suppose."

"Okay, I will get Mike to make space in there, then."

"Mike? Has he been here all day?"

"Yes, he has been great, helping me and chatting with the people who called, even Dennis."

"Dennis was here?" said Alice."

"Yes, but I told him to go, in no uncertain language."

Unknown to Ruth, Mike had made the sitting room ready for the wake. It was just the family there, and they were asked to go to the kitchen while the body was brought in and set up ready for viewing. Mike asked for a word with Alice, and she took him aside to the room off the kitchen where Tom had been sleeping.

He reached for her hands, held them in his, and looked her straight in the face. "I will go now and let you grieve for your husband with your children."

"Call me anytime and I will be here for you." Alice didn't say a word, just put her arms around his neck and hugged him close. Mike kissed her firmly on the lips, turned, and walked out.

The next two days passed in a sort of a blur, with a constant string of people coming and going, some laughter and some tears. In other words, a typical Irish funeral. In a quiet moment alone, Alice sat there and smiled to herself as she wondered what the neighbours would think if they knew that she was hopelessly in love with her farm manager. Should she feel guilty? Maybe, but she didn't.

She did, however, cry genuine tears as they drove out of the yard behind Tom's coffin. He was leaving his beloved farm for the last time with a daughter on either side of her. They shared their grief on his final journey to the church.

It was Eva who broke the silence. "Mam, will we be okay? What will happen to the farm? Will we keep it? What would Dad want?"

"I don't know, sweetheart. I know that we will be okay, no matter what. When you are ready, you and Holly will go back to college. We will have to see Dad's will before we make any decision about the farm."

Chapter 34

Ruth had not heard from Dennis since she ejected him from Connolly's house. She wondered if he was still living with Nancy. She had no ill will towards the woman and almost felt sorry for her. Perhaps she was blissfully happy with Dennis and had no idea that he was trying to dump her. She was sitting halfway down the church beside Mike and was only half listening to all the kind words being said about Tom until Anna Nolan got up to have her say on behalf of the GAA. She talked about Alice and how she supported her husband as he travelled to one meeting after another. Ruth smiled when she thought of the chat they would have at the kitchen table tomorrow.

Everyone at the funeral was invited to the local pub for refreshments after the burial. Mike dropped Ruth off but did not come in. He had work to do. Sarah drove Alice and the girls. Drinks were ordered. Alice was not holding back now and ordered a gin and tonic. The rest of them had wine. People were still coming to shake their hands. She wished that they would stop it now and give them a break.

Ruth was coming back from the ladies' room when she was stopped by a woman she barely knew. The woman had a look of concern. She grabbed her hand and said, "I am so sorry for you, Mrs Cullen. It must have been very difficult for you."

Looking puzzled, Ruth said, "Well, Alice is his wife", thinking that she was referring to Tom.

"No, I am talking about your fella. Bad enough being left for another woman, but a man, that must have been devastating for you." Ruth was speechless. She just stood there, thinking that she was going to faint. The woman was still talking but not being heard. Sarah came on the scene.

"Are you okay?" she asked, and looked at the woman for an answer.

The woman looked embarrassed as she muttered, "Must go", and walked straight out the door.

There was a seat close by, and Sarah steered her friend to sit on it. "What is it, sweetheart? What did she say?"

"She said that Dennis left me for a man." Ruth couldn't utter another word. "Can you take me home, Sarah? I must get out of here."

"Of course I will. Just let me tell Alice that you are ill and must leave."

When they got to the house, Ruth urged Sarah to go back and be with Alice. Eva and Holly had friends there, but Alice would need her.

"Are you sure you'll be okay? Make some hot tea and wrap up well? You have had a massive shock, and who knows, that woman might be talking rubbish. We will work it all out tomorrow." Ruth did as Sarah had suggested, but not with tea. She opened a bottle of wine and poured herself a large glass, wrapped up in a large throw, and sat in her favourite chair. Part of her wanted to ring Dennis and demand the truth. But she couldn't get past the fact that her husband might be gay. How could that be and her not notice it, in all the years that she had been married to him?

It was almost time for her to start her cancer treatment. It was one thing after another. Her mind was racing, remembering how simple things used to be before the holiday. If they had stayed at home, would Tom have died? Would Dennis have left her? Is this what karma looks like?

Ruth was fast asleep in the chair, and when Sarah got home, she decided to let her sleep where she was, noticing the wine glass and the almost-empty bottle beside her. Plus Sarah could not cope with another issue today. Thanks to her boss, she could have a lie-in tomorrow and then talk about Dennis Cullen and his sexuality.

Chapter 35

The Connolly household was quiet for the first time in months. Alice and her daughters sat at the table, a little worse for wear after the drinks the day before.

Eva cried most of the time. "I can't believe that my dad is not coming back."

Holly put her arms around her sister. "Yes, it is going to be difficult for a while", Holly, now crying too, added. "Imagine coming home and dad not being here."

There was a knock at the back door, and Mike entered. Barely putting his head around the kitchen door, he said, "May I come in, ladies?"

Alice said, "Yes, come in, Mike. Will you have a cuppa?"

"Yes, please." As he sat down, it was obvious that he had something to say. "I need to let all three of you know of a conversation I had with Tom a few weeks ago, and I agreed with him. You will probably find it in the will when it is read."

They were all alert now. "Go on, Mike", said Alice.

"Tom was worried about how you all would cope when he was gone, and he talked to me about his plan. It will take some months for probate to happen. In the meantime, he asked me if I would consider staying on to manage the farm, just as I have been doing, until everything is completed." Looking straight at Alice, he said, "And have you decided to keep or sell the farm?"

"Sell the farm?" said Holly. "Mam, are you thinking of selling?"

Alice reached for her daughter's hand. "No, love, I have not thought about it."

Then she addressed both girls. "What do you two think we should do? I won't be able to run it on my own."

It was Mike who interjected. "Ladies, there is no need to concern yourselves with this today. I just wanted you to know that I will continue to work for you until you decide otherwise. Okay, I will get back to work now." Mike stood up to leave.

Alice stood up also. "Why don't you come in for lunch, Mike?"

"Thanks, Alice, but you need some time together now. Another time, okay?" and he left.

Everything looked different today. Mike was now working for the woman he loved, and he longed for some time alone with her to make love to her and talk about the future, their future. He was no longer sure how he was going to fit into her plans. Would she want to stay on the farm or move to Lanzarote with him? One thing was sure: he could not continue to farm for the rest of his life as he was doing now. Even if he sold the pub, it would not be enough to buy Alice out, and he couldn't spend the rest of his time being a farmhand, even if he had the name of manager.

The Connolly girls had to decide if either of them wanted to look after the land or let it go. It was not cost-effective to pay a manager long-term. Holly and Eva had not thought past their father's death, and now they would be forced to decide if they wanted to keep the house and the land and how it would affect their lives.

"I can't imagine not coming home to this house at the weekends", said Eva.

"I know, love", said her mother, "but the farm is not making enough money to provide for the three of us and a manager. Do either of you think that you might want to run the place when you finish college? If you did, I would keep it, but it is not an easy life. Your dad made it look easy because he loved it and never wanted anything else. He had no ambition to make improvements to the house or any such thing".

Alice had said her piece. Now it was up to her children to decide, and thanks to Mike, they had time to come to terms with their new situation. Now she had to decide for herself what she wanted the rest of her life to be. For that she needed Mike. She only knew for sure that she wanted him in it. After that she didn't care. The girls were staying at home for the week, so it was going to be difficult for her to see him alone.

"Typical Alice, just get on with it", thought Sarah. If she only knew that her older sister was just waiting to get the farm manager into her bed, she would be shocked. As if Sarah was reading her mind, she asked, "What happens with Mike now? Are you two going to hook up, or can I have him?" All three laughed.

"Keep your hands off him", said Ruth. "He is spoken for."

"Or is he married?" asked Sarah seriously.

"Not exactly", answered Alice.

Chapter 36

"Any word from Dennis", asked Sarah?

"Not a word."

"Well, then, Mrs Cullen, you and I need to do some detective work."

Ruth looked shocked. What do you mean, detective work?

"We will go to Carlow, watch him come out from work, and follow him home to Nancy or Ned or whomever. We need to know who is telling the truth and who is lying. Seeing is believing, and you can't decide what to do without the facts."

Being careful not to stay too close to his car, but close enough to see Dennis coming out of his office and then following him to see where he was living, and above all who he was living with? This must have been a first, a wife waiting to see if her husband was with a man or a woman. What sort of woman would not know such basic things about the man she had lived with for so long?

Ruth was a nervous wreck by the time he came out and went to his car. On his own, he got in and drove away.

Sarah followed him into Carlow town. He parked outside a small hotel and went in. Looking from one to the other, Sarah said, "What now?"

"I don't know. I have never had to do this before."

"Let's just wait and see if he comes out again. Could he be living here?"

"I suppose it is possible, but who is he with, and is it male or female?

"Sarah, I think that is the big question. I almost hope he is with a woman. Otherwise, I have been living with a gay man all these years and couldn't see it. What does that say about me?"

"It is all on him. You are innocent in this situation, Ruth."

"Innocent!" thought Ruth. "I am hardly that." Remembering Danni, lying on the bed, his beautiful naked body beside her, she had never looked at Dennis like that, never longed for his touch.

Suddenly, she didn't care who he was with. She just knew that they were not getting back together. "Okay, Sarah, let us go home."

Sarah was shocked. "What do you mean? We don't know what he is doing in there."

"I know, and I don't care if he is with a man or a woman. I just know that he is not coming back to me, not now or ever again. I am better on my own than being with someone I don't trust."

Sarah started the car and began to drive out of the space opposite the hotel when Ruth saw him leaving, on his own. She said nothing to her friend as they drove away. "I will ring him later and tell him that it is over. Then he can take all his stuff and go his own way. I can hardly believe that I was thinking of having him back. Let's go to see Alice and the girls. And, Sarah, thank you for doing this for me. I feel so much better now that the decision is made."

Sarah and Ruth arrived; it was a welcome distraction for Alice. The girls had some friends in the kitchen, so they retired to the sitting room. "What are you two up to?" laughed Alice, sensing that something was going on with them.

"We were doing some detective work", laughed Sarah. She put her arms around her sister and hugged her closely. "How are you, Sis?"

"I am okay. I just must get on with it."

"Sarah", started Alice, "it is time that you got the truth from me."

"Would you like me to go?" asked Ruth.

"No, not at all." Alice opened a bottle of wine and poured three glasses.

"You see, Sis, I met Mike in Lanzarote, and that's how he came to be working here."

Sarah stood up, keeping the glass in her hand. "What! I thought he came from Galway?"

Alice was struggling now. "Come back and sit down, Sarah. Yes, he is from Galway, but he has a bar down in Lanzarote. That's how we met him."

"We! So you are in on this, too?" She looked suspiciously at Ruth.

"Yes, Sarah, it was all my idea. Mike Wall told us how he had to leave the land and find another way to make a living. We both liked him, and when Tom needed someone to look after the farm, I contacted Mike, and he said yes."

"Hold on now! A stranger you met on holiday came here to help Alice, leaving his own business to do this. Am I missing something?"

They looked from one to the other, wondering what to say next. It had to be Alice who spoke, or leave the rest of the story for another time. Alice said, "Another glass, anyone?" and she refilled all three glasses.

"Okay, I may as well get this out of the way. Sarah, Mike and I did more than talk; we fell in love."

"Love, sure, you were only there for a few days."

"A lot can happen in a few days, Sarah. You saw Tom and me. Do you think we loved each other?"

"How would I know? You were just Tom and Alice. You were like most couples who have been married for a lifetime."

"Yes! And let me tell you, little sister, that is not a good place to be, and, yes, I am sorry for the girls that he died, but I would have left him to be with Mike."

Chapter 37

It was two days before Dennis turned up with a bag. Ruth asked him to sit down; time to be honest with each other. "I was told that you left me to be with a man." He was about to answer, but Ruth raised her hand. "Dennis, I don't know or care if it was a man, a woman, or anything else. The fact is that you left and you are not coming back."

He looked like he might cry. "But what am I supposed to do? I have no place to go."

"Go back to wherever you have been since you left here. Go to the moon for all I care. I don't love you, and I don't trust you, Dennis Cullen. So take your bag and go; let me know when you want to collect the rest of your stuff." She held the door open as her husband walked out for the last time.

She stood in the living room of the home they shared for twenty years, her chair, his chair, photos and memories of good times they shared. "What now?" She was single again at forty-nine, and questions would be asked. "Where is he?" "Who is he with?" "Are you getting divorced?" And many more. However, first things first, radiation therapy.

It was decided that Alice would drive Ruth on the first day of treatment and see how she was feeling afterwards. External beam radiation would not be too severe, or so they were told, but they didn't know of anyone who had been through it. Alice sat in the waiting room and said a silent prayer for her friend; she prayed more recently that things would turn out right for her children and herself and Mike. It was not long before Ruth emerged, none the worse for the treatment. This became routine for the next four days until Friday. Then a nurse sat beside them and explained that they would take a break. She could continue to go to work, but only if she felt well enough. Do your usual stuff, but don't push yourself. Take a rest when you need to. Remember, you have nothing to prove to anyone. "Just one question", said Ruth. The nurse nodded. "Can I have a glass or two of wine?"

"Of course you can, and enjoy it."

There was a sense of relief after the first week of treatment. Alice came into the house for a coffee when she dropped Ruth home. Sarah had gone back to her own home now, and they could talk freely.

Ruth carried two cups of coffee to the dining table, and they sat in silence for a short time. Alice had a grin on her face as she said, "I think we need a holiday". There was a burst of laughter. They had not done that for what seemed like ages, and it felt good.

"If you could go back in time, would you change anything?" asked Ruth. Alice thought about it. "Are you talking about Mike?"

"Yes."

"I wouldn't change a thing where that man is concerned, and I can't wait to spend Christmas with him. I hope you will be there with us? I plan to let the girls know about Mike and me during the holidays."

"Oh", said Ruth. "How do you think that will go down?"

"I'm not sure, but they need to know before they go back to Dublin. Then they will have time to process the new situation, and Mike and I can get on with our lives."

"Thanks, Alice, that sounds nice, although I have to say that Christmas is not something on my mind this year. I know it's just around the corner, but I don't feel it. Too much has changed this year, and my head is all over the place. I feel like going into bed and coming out again when it's all over."

Later that night, while sitting at home, Ruth came to a decision. She would go to a hotel for a few days and ignore Christmas. Straight away, she got on her computer and began looking for places to stay. A quiet country hotel with a pool, perhaps, and areas close by for long walks. Within the hour, she had found the perfect place, so she booked it. Her first big decision, now that she was on her own, was how it must be from now on. She would be leaving on December 23. No need to worry about Alice. She had Sarah, Mike, and her two daughters. This was about herself and the end of this year and all the misery that had come into her life. She had no mind for celebrating anything.

Chapter 38

Unlike Ruth, Alice was making plans for the festive season, and Mike was up to speed on his part and how they would gently let the girls know that they were together, without making a big announcement. He would help her with cooking dinner and decorating the table. They would not put the tree up this year, as a way of showing the girls that their father was remembered.

Mike was to stay in the house but not in Alice's room. They would make that clear, again without saying it. Everything had to run smoothly. As much as she wanted Mike, her daughters should not feel like their father had been replaced so quickly. It was decided that a decision on the farm would be made at Easter.

Sarah arrived early on Christmas Day, laden with presents for everyone, even Ruth. Alice was sworn to secrecy about Ruth's plan to disappear for the duration. Except for Mike, no one knew where she was. Alice just told them that Ruth was not able to face Christmas this year but there was no need to worry about her.

Holly and Eva didn't seem at all surprised to have Mike in the house on Christmas Day. He made himself busy in the background, cooking breakfast and later preparing vegetables for the main meal. After the meal, the girls planned to visit friends close by. Sarah also planned to visit friends. Leaving Mike and Alice at home, Holly asked if her mam was okay to be left at home. Mike answered, "Don't worry, girls, I will be here to keep her company". As he spoke, he crossed the room and sat on the couch beside Alice.

His move wasn't wasted on the young women. They nudged each other and laughed. "Mam, are you sure that you are safe with Mike?"

Alice laughed, too. "Go on, off with yourselves, and have a good time. We will be okay."

Sarah decided to take her to leave at the same time. Just looking at the pair on the couch, she said, "Be good, you two".

Finally alone, Mike reached for Alices hand. He lifted it and kissed it, his lips lingering there until she lifted her other hand and placed it on his face. Their eyes met, and the passion between them was overflowing. Without a word, they stood up, holding hands, and made their way upstairs. They each began to undress the other, slowly, while their passion burned within. They lay on the bed, not under the bedclothes, and Mike made gentle put passionate love to her.

They got into bed and cuddled up. Alice couldn't be happier. She was so lucky to have met Mike. Otherwise, she was sure that she would never have this overwhelming urge for sex ever again. She and Tom never experienced this feeling; sex had always felt like something that had to be done just to get it over with.

Neither one wanted to leave the comfort of each other's arms, but Alice worried that if she went to sleep and the girls came home, they might look in to see if she was okay. They had to stick to the plan. They went back downstairs and had a glass of wine at the kitchen table. Reaching for her hand again, Mike looked pleadingly at Alice. "When can we tell them, so that we can be together properly? I want to spend the rest of my life with you, Alice Connolly."

"Oh! Mr Wall, that sounds like a proposal", laughed Alice. With that, Mike stood up and walked to the other side of the table, went down on one knee, and asked her to marry him. She cupped his face with both hands and said yes.

"Now, do you need help to get up out of there?"

Mike laughed. "Yes, please." They hugged and kissed like a pair of kids, both smiling widely.

Chapter 39

Ruth had found what looked like the perfect place to hide away from the merry-making and endless love longs. It was a country house in Wicklow, not too far away, but it was open for the duration of the festive season. It was difficult to ignore the decorations and lights everywhere. At least they were not in her room. It was beautifully furnished with a lot of old-world charm, as you would expect in an old country house.

The view from her room was beautiful. There was a lake and what looked like a walkway around it. It made her want to get out there in the cold December air, and that is what she did. Delighted with her warm walking boots, which were barely worn up to now, dressed in her winter woollies, she made her way downstairs. There it was again, Christmas. There was no getting away from it, until she walked out the front door of the hotel.

Ruth put a light pair of shoes into her car so that if her boots were mucky, she didn't have to walk into the hotel wearing them. "Good thinking", she thought as she smiled to herself. The hotel grounds were perfect for her, especially around the lake, but it was a constant battle between admiring the beauty of nature and her thoughts. There was a seat halfway around the lake. It looked like a good place to sit and take in the full view.

What would she do when this was over, move away from Ballycastle? Start a new life? Sell the house? Remembering what Dennis had said about not wanting his half of the house, she wondered now if he had changed his mind. Either way, the house was no longer a home, and the memories were more like nightmares. Alice would be starting her new life with Mike. Suddenly she felt lonely, and there was a lump in her throat. Tears began to stream down her face, wishing now that she had children. That would be a reason to go on.

Despite her warm clothes, Ruth felt cold inside and out, and no amount of clothes would change that. Perhaps if she had some food, it might help. On the walk back to the hotel, her phone rang. It was Alice. Time to put on a brave face. "Yes, I got here. It is beautiful. Just out for a walk and going back now for dinner." No need to mention dinner and a bottle of wine in her room. That would just upset her friend, and Alice deserved a bit of happiness after the time she had had.

Dinner arrived, beautifully laid out on a tray. The waiter asked if she wanted the tray collected. "No thank you. I will leave it out." She gave him a tip, and she was alone. The meal looked lovely, but she just picked at it, sitting by the window looking out, a glass of wine in her hand. "I wonder where Dennis is?" It was just a brief thought. A text arrived, but her phone was beside the bed. She thought, "Oh, fuck off", knowing it wasn't Alice.

The wine was nice, and the food was going down very slowly. Ruth liked her food, but not in her present state. The phone sounded again, so she got up to look at it. She didn't recognise the number, but it said, "Feliz Navidad Amor". Her heart beat so fast. "It is him." She had almost no Spanish, but these words she did know, from a song. It seemed like a long time since Danni, but the memories hadn't faded and never would.

Should she answer or not? He was bound to have moved on by now. Men like him were never short of beautiful women, and young ones at that. Danni Garcia could have any woman he wanted, and remembering how he liked sex, it was best left in the past. This was time to think about her future. Sitting there on the luxurious bed, she was tempted to climb into it. Just another glass of wine to kill the pain.

How had it come to this? Was it Danni? Or the holiday? Or Dennis? Then there was radiation therapy and Tom Connolly dying. If only one could go back and change things. She and Dennis had been doing okay. Then she remembered him saying that he had been with the other woman for a while. That was not her fault; he was having an affair behind her back. Another gulp of wine. He was probably going to leave her anyway.

Chapter 40

Somewhere between drinking and crying, Ruth fell asleep, still fully dressed, apart from her shoes. She went from sitting on the side of the bed to moving into the middle of it and curling up into the foetal position. It was dawn when she woke up feeling cold. It was time to get into bed. Worn out she drifted off again, into a deep sleep this time, knowing that she could sleep for as long as she wanted to and order food whenever she felt like it.

"Miss Cullen, you have a visitor." It was the house phone, and Ruth had answered it without thinking, and she was barely awake anyway.

"Yes, I'm sorry. What did you say?"

"There is a gentleman here to see you."

"I'm sorry, that must be a mistake. No one knows where I am. Hold on, I will ring you back."

Danni sat at reception. He planned to surprise her, but now he wondered if he had made a mistake. Mike told him where she was hiding out for Christmas, and he felt sure that if he met her, she would spend some time with him.

He had not been able to get her out of his mind since they met, but now he was not so sure.

"Alice, did you tell Dennis where I was staying?"

"No, Ruth, no. Why do you ask?"

"Reception just told me that there is a man downstairs to see me. I have to ask, did you tell Mike?"

"Sorry, yes, I did."

"Could he have told anyone? Please ask him."

Alice came back to say that he had told Danni Garcia when he asked whom she was spending Christmas with. "I am so sorry, Ruth. It never dawned on me that this could happen."

"Surely, he didn't fly from Lanzarote today. Oh my God, could it be him? What am I going to do, Alice?"

"Do you want to see him?"

"I didn't think I would ever set eyes on him again, so I blocked him out of my mind."

"Well, if he has come all this way, you had better at least talk to him on the phone. He deserves that much."

"Okay, I will do that. Thanks, Alice."

"Hello, Danni, where are you?"

When she heard his voice, her heart jumped. "I am at your hotel, hoping that you will speak with me."

Ruth laughed. "Yes, of course I will, but I must shower and get dressed."

"Okay, I will check in, and you phone me when you are ready."

"Imagine, Danni is here in this hotel just to see me. Good God, it's Christmas Eve. What will I wear?" She showered, all the time giggling to herself like a schoolgirl. She couldn't waste time thinking about what she would wear, so pulling on her jeans and a jumper, it was time to see him.

He knocked on her door, and her heart was beating faster than usual. He looked different in his warm clothes but just as handsome. Ruth went into his outstretched arms, and he hugged her so tight, the smell of him brought all the memories flooding back. She wanted him to kiss her, but he didn't. Moving her back slightly, he asked, "What would you like to do, Ruth?" Even how he said her name excited her.

"Let's walk and chat." They walked around the lake. Danni had never been to Ireland before and was taking note of the beauty all around him. He didn't seem as self-assured now as he did when they met first. When they got to the halfway seat, they sat down.

"Now, Miss Ruth, tell me why you are hiding away out here for the holidays. What are you running away from?" He was quiet then, giving her time to tell all. He was holding her hand, and it made her feel safe. He never once interrupted her, all through the story of the end of her marriage and the decision to run away from Christmas. They continued the walk around the lake in relative silence.

Now Ruth didn't need to hide from the lights and the music. The Christmas tree looked beautiful, and they sat by the fire in the lobby and had two hot whiskeys. "Now, Mr Garcia, what made you come all the way up from Lanzarote to find me?"

"Well", began Danni, "it is a problem with my heart".

Ruth was startled. "Your heart?"

"Yes", he laughed. "It was broken when you left and then would not take my calls. Thank God I had Mike to let me know that you got through your treatment okay and that you have good friends looking after you. But I wanted to do all that for you, and you wouldn't even speak to me."

"But, Danni, we were a summer fling. Nobody expects that to last."

He looked at her sadly now. "Is that all I am to you? A fling, you call it. Ruth, I fell in love with you." With that, he stood up and walked towards the stairs. The light on the tree didn't look so bright now. How was she going to get him back. He must not walk out of her life now, and it was up to her to stop him.

The receptionist kindly gave her some note paper and an envelope, and Ruth began her first-ever love letter.

Danni,

Please don't leave without talking to me. You left without hearing my side and how I feel about you. When I said "a fling", that meant a holiday romance, and that is what I thought we had. I never believed for one second that you might want to see me again. You swept me off my feet when I met you, and I had to try to control my feelings for you, to save me from a broken heart when we had to say goodbye, and I left for home, and you moved on to the next woman. I am so sorry, but that is how I saw it. I cried as the flight took off, and my heart was broken at the thought of never seeing you again, never being kissed or loved as we did. I didn't think it was possible that you might love me or feel anything of what I felt.

You coming here today tells me that I was wrong about you, and when we walked hand in hand earlier, it was like walking on air, and the world looked good. I want you in my life, Danni. Don't go.

Love,
Ruth XXX

She asked for his room number only to be told that it couldn't be given out. "Okay. I will leave it with you and tell him to pick it up."

The receptionist took a call. "Yes, sir. I will call a taxi straight away, but it will be at least thirty-five minutes."

Ruth handed her the letter addressed to Mr Garcia and went to her room. She texted him, "I have left a letter for you at reception. Please read it, and then let's talk. XX".

Sitting on the bed watching her phone and at the same time waiting for a knock at her door, time passed quickly. If she went out, she might miss him. Why wasn't he answering her text? "I can't believe that he came all this way to be with me and now over a silly word, we are separated again. He will be back", she told herself. An hour had passed and not a word. Ruth pulled on a black dress, a pair of heels, and some jewellery and went downstairs to wait for him. "Surely, he will come down for dinner", she thought, taking a chair facing the staircase. "Now I can't miss him."

Thirty-five minutes later, and with one glass of wine, it was time to ask if he had picked up her letter. As she approached the desk, there was a different person on duty. Even before she asked, she could see her letter exactly where it was left. "Hello, I left a letter for Mr Garcia."

"Oh", said the young man. "I am sorry, but Mr Garcia has checked out." Ruth wanted to shout at him and call him all the names that were in her mind. What now?

"Time for another glass of wine. He won't get a flight at this time on Christmas Eve, so he must still be in Ireland." Then she remembered who could contact him, and she had to try to get him back. Mike would talk sense into him. After a long conversation with Mike and telling him how she felt, Mike agreed to call him.

Looking around at couples all dressed up and taking photos in front of the Christmas tree, Ruth said a prayer that she would get another chance at the happiness she felt earlier with Danni. Normally Ruth Cullen would feel self-conscious sitting in the foyer of a hotel all dressed up and all alone, but not now. It didn't matter. Only one thing mattered: Would he give her another chance? Ordering another glass of wine from a passing waiter seemed like the only thing to do. At least it would dull the pain.

"Your wine, madame."

"Thank you", said Ruth without even looking up, and then the waiter sat down beside her. She looked at him, in surprise, and then did a second take. It was Danni.

"How did you get in without me seeing you?"

There were no words. He leaned over and kissed her, a long, lingering kiss that said everything. When it ended, he looked at her adoringly. "You look beautiful, Ruth. I do love you and will for the rest of my life." They just sat there holding hands.

After a while Danni ordered a drink, Irish whiskey. "I will try to catch up with you." Ruth didn't want to spend too much time drinking, she wanted him in her bed, but he made her wait. He was savouring just being with her and being in Ireland for the first time.

Chapter 41

"I feel so happy", said Ruth. "I want to ring Alice and tell her."

Danni caught her hand. "No, please. I just want us to be alone for the moment. We have things to talk about." Ruth looked questioningly at him. "Yes, like where will we live, here or there? Have you ever considered living in Lanzarote?"

"Okay", she thought, as she remembered that Danni had a daughter, but she would have to leave her friends. The house no longer mattered to her. What would she do to earn a living?

"No, I haven't, but I will now, have you thought it through? Yes, I have. I came here to find you and to someday make you my wife, but I can't decide for you, Ruth."

"Okay, let us just enjoy Christmas and being here together.

Squeezing her hand, Danni said, "Let's see if the magic between us is still there." Ruth could feel the magic the moment she saw him again. "Would you like to dance?"

"With you, yes, please." He caught her hand and led her to the dance floor, and she was so glad now that she had packed her black dress. The band was playing "White Christmas", and Danni put one strong arm around her and held her hand in the other as they began to move with the music. He danced so well. Then the Spanish were known to be good dancers. Ruth thought that all the women in the room must be jealous of her.

They ended the evening with a beautiful meal and a bottle of wine. She knew that he was making her wait. She could hardly eat with anticipation of what was coming. When the meal was finished, he asked if she would like to go for a stroll. Looking him straight in the face, she said no. "I want you to make love to me, now. I can't wait any longer." They both laughed.

He took her face between his hands and kissed her. "I had to be sure that you felt the same as me."

Ruth never remembered being so happy. It was Christmas Day when they finally collapsed in each other's arms and slept. She never wanted to be without this man again. When she opened her eyes and saw him there, her heart was bursting with pleasure. It was the first time they had slept all night together. She moved slightly, and Danni opened his eyes.

"I was afraid that you might have disappeared and it was all just a lovely dream." He laughed. "Happy Christmas, my love", he whispered as he kissed her.

Then he put his hand under the pillow and took out a small box wrapped in festive paper. Ruth sat up in the bed and opened it. It was a very beautiful ring, an emerald surrounded by diamonds. She was aghast. "You like it?"

"Yes, I love it, and it fits. Thank you so much, Danni. I wish I had something to give to you."

"You have. All that I could ever want is for you to say that we have a future together."

Neither of them wanted to get out of bed. It was Danni who insisted. "Come on, we have the rest of our lives to make love. Let's go and join in the fun, our first Christmas together."

"The rest of our lives. Okay, I will go with that", thought Ruth. As they descended the staircase, everything looked beautiful, and it felt like the perfect Christmas, with Danni Garcia holding her hand. The day passed so quickly as they talked about each other's lives from childhood and how they got to where they are now.

Danni got a one-way flight, not knowing if he was going to be turned down and returning home alone or coming back with Ruth. He had a manager in the restaurant for a week. Now he had to think about coming to live in Ireland long term and how to tell his daughter, who was spending the holidays with her mother.

Ruth was struggling with the idea of living in Lanzarote. She loved it in her short time there, but hated the thought of leaving Alice, Sarah, her job, and all the familiar things around her. Then she remembered that she could not speak Spanish, except for a few words. Alice would be struggling now until she had the farm sorted. It was the worst possible time to leave her.

It was time for a chat with Alice. Danni agreed, and they left the hotel and went back to her house in Barrycastle. On the journey, Danni was confused by the traffic on the other side of the road. It would be strange for either of them to make the move, and they talked about the pros and cons all the way down.

It was mid-afternoon when they arrived at the Connelly home. Alice and the girls were there waiting patiently to meet Ruth's Spanish lover. Mike had told them about Danni, what a good man he was, and how he had fallen in love with Ruth.

Even though it was Saint Stephens Day, the animals still had to be looked after, and Mike was out on the farm doing what needed to be done. Alice hugged her friend. "Look at you, radiant after a few days away."

They hugged again and laughed together, before Alice turned her attention to Danni. She held her hand out to greet him, and he held her hand and leaned in to kiss her on both cheeks, in Spanish style. "Alice, it is good to see you", Danni told her.

The two young girls stood watching Danni. Holly nudged her sister and giggled. "I would take him any day over Dennis Cullen".

"Yes, he is gorgeous, and the accent is to die for."

Before going into the house, Alice introduced him to her daughters. Danni asked for Mike.

"He is out on the farm", said Alice. "He will be in later for dinner. You two can chat then. You two will stay for dinner, won't you?"

"Thank you, Alice. That would be great", said Ruth. "What time are you planning to eat?"

"About seven", answered Alice. "Okay, we will go to my place and drop off our bags then and come back."

Chapter 42

Ruth began the short, familiar drive to her house. She still found it difficult to believe that Danni Garcia was sitting next to her going to the house that she had lived in since she married Dennis all those years ago. When they arrived and took their bags inside, Danni sensed her mood. He stood there in the living room and put his strong arms around her, and she felt safe. "Don't worry, my love. We will work it out." He lifted her head slightly and their lips came together, gently at first, and their passion grew. Moments later Ruth led the way to the bedroom and all decisions were forgotten.

They lay there in the bed, their bodies moulded together. It was Danni who broke the silence. "I don't like this house." Ruth looked up at him with a question mark on her face. Danni continued, "He slept here with you, and I hate that, and he didn't know how special you are".

She moved up to his face and kissed him. "I love you". He laughed. "Stop it now Ruth, we have to go for dinner", she kissed him again. And they both laughed.

On the way back to Alice's. Ruth declared, "I have made a decision."

Danni looked puzzled. "Go on", he said.

"I am going to sell the house and leave that part of my life behind me."

Mike was in the kitchen when they arrived, and Alice was busy with dinner. The two men greeted each other as old friends. Ruth went to help Alice. "The girls are gone out and won't be home, thankfully", said Alice with a giggle. "We are free, well, for tonight anyway."

They all sat down to roast beef with all the trimmings. Alice stretched out her hand to show off her ring. Mike proposed, and I accepted. Reaching for her hand, Mike said, "This is the only woman I ever wanted to marry. If she didn't come along, I would have died a bachelor". Ruth and Danni clapped for both of them, and then they all raised their glasses to toast Alice and Mike. Not wanting to take from their celebrations, Ruth turned her new ring around.

Mike asked Danni about when he arrived and if he was planning to return to Lanzarote soon. "We haven't decided yet what we are going to do, except for Alice. She has made a decision, and I am hoping that it is looking good for me." The two women noticed that he was speaking for them as a couple. Alice looked questionably at her friend, for confirmation. Ruth nodded. Alice reached across and squeezed her hand.

So Mike said, "What is this decision, Ruth?"

"I am going to sell the house and start afresh", she answered. "I am going back with Danni and see how it goes."

Danny stood up, reached down, and caught her hand to raise her up. He hugged her tightly. "Young lady, you have made me the happiest man alive. I will do everything I can to see that you are happy. Looking her straight in the eye, he said, "You will never be taken for granted again".

"I was worried about leaving you at this time." Ruth was looking at Alice. "But seeing you with this good man, I have no worries now."

"Fantastic", said Mike. "I think I have a job for you in Lanzarote."

Ruth was all ears. "A job for me?"

"Yes", answered Mike. "You will oversee my place while we get around to making decisions. Danni will show you the ropes. You can do it together."

Ruth's eyes filled up, and tears of joy rolled down her face. Alice saw it and asked her for help with dessert, to give her time to compose herself. Alice put her arms around her. "Come on, now", Alice said. "Is this happiness or shock?"

"Both", answered Ruth. "Things are happening so fast and changing so much." She dried her eyes. "But in a good way. I am so happy, Alice."

The End

About the Author

Tessa Daly hails from Co. Waterford in Ireland. Just Harmless Flirting is her second novella. A Parrish Affair is her first.

A Parrish Affair
Ciara Parrish finally found the life she spent years dreaming of. She had an adoring husband willing to do everything to keep her happy. She lived a charmed life in the quiet town of Ballyfauna, Ireland and life was good. Ciare had it all. Or so she thought.

The first cracks appeared not long after her new boss took over. Fr David Magee was everything his predecessor was not; witty, attractive, and driven. It wasn't until his flirting left Ciara breathless that she realized she had a problem. Making matters worse, she was unable to keep David away from her personal life. Jealousy flares as her husband starts to conjure dark thoughts.

Determined to stop their too cosy friendship from developing further, he spreads a vicious rumor that spirals out of control and threatens to undo everything in their lives. Can Ciara find it in her heart to forgive him and will she ever be happy again?

Please Review

Dear Reader,

If you enjoyed this book, I would really appreciate if you could leave a review on Amazon or Goodreads. Your opinion counts and it does influence buyer decision on whether to purchase the book or not. Thank You!

                                                                      Tessa

www.ingramcontent.com/pod-product-compliance
Lightning Source LLC
Chambersburg PA
CBHW030300100526
44590CB00012B/460